December 21, 2021

Waking Up to

Connecticut Poets in a Time

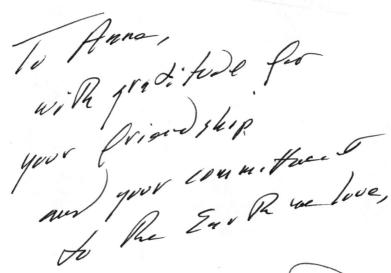

To Anna,
with gratitude for
your friendship
and your commitment
to the Earth we love,

Love, ...

Blessing you with this book!

Waking Up to the Earth
Connecticut Poets in a Time of Global Climate Crisis

Margaret Gibson, Editor

First Readers: David K. Leff and Rhonda M. Ward
Editorial Advisors: Marilyn Nelson and Bessy Reyna

Funded by a grant to State Poet Laureate Margaret Gibson
by the Academy of American Poets

Grayson Books | West Hartford, Connecticut | graysonbooks.com

Waking Up to the Earth: Connecticut Poets in a Time of Global Climate Crisis
Copyright © 2021 Margaret Gibson
ISBN: 978-1-7335568-8-0
Published by Grayson Books
West Hartford, Connecticut

Library of Congress Control Number: 2020951134

Interior and Cover Design: Cindy Stewart
Cover Art: "Pamet Marsh Reeds" by Jon Friedman, in the collection of Rick Cotton
and Elizabeth Smith

Contents

Introduction

Poets have always written about the earth, about their local habitation. In their own particular and indigenous words and images, poets say where they are, who they are, and what else lives with them in their surrounding world, be it terrestrial or oceanic, forested or plain, ice-bound or tropical. And poets, perhaps more than others, think about the roots of words, discovering that many words themselves, when one considers their origins, bind us to the earth.

The word *climate*, for instance descends to us from a Greek word *klima*, which meant "the sloping surface of the earth." Knowing the root of that word makes all the difference to me when I say, "global climate crisis." I think of the slope of the earth, earth on a slippery slope. I lose my balance.

Language can also separate; the mind can divide. The word *crisis*, as I have written elsewhere,[i] "descends from the Greek word *krinen: to separate, to judge.*" (Its earlier Indo-European root echoes the act of sieving.) We human beings can disregard commonality and interrelationship; we can and do separate ourselves from the others—and we often live in an egotistic isolation. And this way of living has consequences: *Crisis.*

The poems in *Waking Up to the Earth* are written by poets who are waking up and paying closer attention to the earth. Mindfulness, as David Hinton describes it, is "that attentiveness to things at hand that enable us to inhabit our lives with immediacy as a rich and profound experience."[ii] And what these poets in their different ways are waking up to is the close kinship between poetry and ecology,[iii] both of which focus on interrelationship. A poem weaves a web of related thoughts and rhythms and images; an eco-system is all about interdependence and the energetic relationship of all sentient beings.

The poems in this anthology are written by poets who are waking up to the root of the word *ecology; oikos* means house or home. These poems call us home to ourselves as human inhabitants who are not separate from the other inhabitants on this earth, who will flourish or be injured not alone, but with others. Everything is connected, kin, interrelated. What we do, how we think, how we sing, how we build, how we fish or harvest from the sea or land, how we construct our cities—all of it matters. In a few poems in this collection, the poets put their hands directly into the earth, the soil, the humus from which comes the word *humility*. All of the poems offer us a vision of human beings who seek to have a more humble relationship with the earth.

A poem from the Modoc tradition, brief and distilled, goes like this: "I/the song/I walk here." I imagine a man or woman out walking in the surrounding environment, mind so open, so empty of thought and distraction, that hearing the song of a bird, the listener becomes the bird. Try to imagine a rapture like that, a selflessness like that—both grounded and fully present. In our lives such unitive moments are few, and most everything in our industrialized, secular culture pushes us away from moments of interrelationship. Each poet in *Waking Up to the Earth* is, however, moving in that direction.

Waking Up to the Earth is organized by poem, not by poet. There is a loosely knit grouping of poems, but no division by section, no separation. If you follow the "trail map" of the poems, you will begin with poems that venture out mindfully to pay attention to "the other," be that a raven or a dung beetle, an owl or a whale, an oak or an aspen. In many poems there is the bright lens of praise; in others the lens is darkened by the threat of extinctions. The map winds through fauna and flora, through forests and waters of all sorts: river, ocean, rainstorm. The trail map takes us through backyards, city parks, urban landscapes. A few poems make the connection between environmental injustice and social or racial injustice. Along the way, certain poems broaden the perspective to a more global one.

There are only a few poems in the collection which speak about "doing" something, taking action to repair the greed and the disregard that leads to climate crisis. It is certainly true that seeing is an action, that witness is an action, and that language anchors one's vision of the earth. But there is also the need for social action. At the close of the collection there are poems which meditate on the unthinkable but possible end result of climate change as it tips into crisis and as crisis tips into the end of the earth as we know it. Unless... Unless we change our lives.

Chase Twichell, an eloquent poet, born and raised in New Haven, Connecticut, now living elsewhere, has said in her poem "Touch Me Not" (published in *The Ghost of Eden*) that she knows the earth will continue in some form. But then comes her outcry: "But I love this one."

The poets in *Waking Up to the Earth* love this one.

I am grateful to all the poets in this collection for their vision and voice. I am grateful to all the many other poets who sent poems for consideration; although they couldn't be included, each poem had merit and conviction. And to all of us, this invitation: Let's keep waking up to the earth and to each other. Let's keep writing poems of eloquent attention and witness. Poetry allows us to wake up and to see; it teaches us how to sustain our gaze, paying attention, even when it may hurt to see.

—Margaret Gibson

i. Margaret Gibson, "Listening to the Thrush: Notes toward the Greening of Poetry in a Time of Global Climate Change," *Georgia Review*, Fall, 2020.

ii. David Hinton, *The Wilds of Poetry*, 2017.

iii. Roger Deakin, *Wild Wood: A Journey Through Tree*, 2007.

The Poems

Walking with Ruskin

Robert Cording

Each day I walk for an hour or two,
what started as exercise now a matter
of devotion. Or, less grandly:
walking gives me something to do,
a kind of discipline since I don't know
how to move towards any of those
big intangible goals—wholeness, God,
forgiveness, justice—but I know how
to walk. Sometimes I bring Ruskin along.

Despite his holy striving and cloying
superlatives ("the greatest thing
a human soul does in the world is
to see something," or "art springs from
the most profound admiration"),
I like the way he forgets himself
in his concern for what is particular
about an eagle's beak or the green-brown
coppery iridescence of a pheasant's feather.

He's teaching me a kind of readiness
for what comes along as it pleases:
a line of ants carrying the remains
of a red emerald butterfly, or
a brook in winter moving under ice
like the one-celled life found in a drop
of water under a microscope.
I like to compare notes with him,
to count the shades of blue

on a kingfisher's back or the three
different kinds of wing feathers,
but I'm still learning to look at things
with Ruskin's respect for fact
and his love for what's being seen—
this beetle, say, that's crossed our path,
its two topside eyes ringed in white,

the lacquer of its shell a depth
of black and darkest greens.

Today, the late July pond water looks
like used car oil, and the roadside grass
is a pointillist study of greens
and the bright white coffee cups of
Americans who run on Dunkin'.
Ruskin and I are looking at clouds,
a kind of medicine. Ruskin says,
they *calm and purify*, if only because
the sky is large and we are not.

And if I'm always half-thinking of
my credit card debt, or if I'm seven
to ten years of mortgaged life
away from retirement, I go on
crouching down for a beetle
that doesn't care if it's seen, though
my seeing it makes the day more real
to me. Nothing much, but something
I'm always thanking Ruskin for.

Luna Moths

Robert Cording

The first time I woke up crying
from a puddle of sleep and found it

fluttering against a wall
like a dying leaf of spring green light.

The second I found lying lightly
on the ground, newly dead.

I brought it inside, and placed it
on a blank piece of paper

for my study. Palest green wings.
A thin red border, like a child's outline,

on the edges of its forewings
and hindwings. A yellow inner border

on its long, tailed hindwings.
Four white eyespots, ringed in yellow

and maroon. On that white
sheet of paper, it appeared to be

some lost metaphor
of an indecipherable language.

**

I'd read the facts—the one-week life span,
the way, because they do not eat,

the adults have no need of a mouth—by the time
I found the third, late at night

high on the wall of my kitchen.
I'd had too much to drink. I spoke to it

as if it were my own Buddhist teacher
here to teach me non-attachment,

the illusions of hunger, sex, rampant need.
I sat with it until the sun rose, toasting

its quick beauty, then the restfulness I found
in its body, and then those bright-eyed,

translucent green wings that seemed
to breathe more and more slowly before going

motionless. When I lifted it in my hand
I knew just how little the space was

between myself and nothingness.

Ravens in Winter

Carol Chaput

Floating between earth's plane and sky's arch,
a smudge, then a thickening of two or more.
Their calls are prayers, like lightning. The Old Ones say
the flap of their wings calls forth thunder's clap.
No wonder we fall to our knees as they wing along
the edge of the sky over wind-scrubbed fields,
always knowing where they are by the smell of grasses
and how wind waves through crowns of trees.
Weightless, they fall in a spill of cinders, of carbon
shadows, to the marsh, filling up everything that's empty and
calling back and forth until the point of stillness.
Always on the edge of my mind, watching the swoop,
the dive, the soar, and sun, wanting what Icarus wanted—
no horizon, no boundary.

The Turtle

Cortney Davis

Not quite crushed by the car,
she waited, the intricate tile of her shell
cracked open, exposing
the deep red of liver, shiny globe
of lung, a string of tissue
pulled out by the eggs
that popped from her on impact.
The soft-white insides, webbed
with a net of vessels, still pulsed.

She was an old turtle, old friend,
trying to dig her nest in the driveway.

She held up her head while her thick
clawed feet swam in the gravel
and she turned to see who
was kneeling beside her. It took such
a long time, sun and ants called by blood,
small gnats to be kept away
from the warm smell of her.

The sun went down in a humid fog
and still she moved when touched.
Her eyes sank a little
into the green leather of her face—
she scanned the world as if to memorize
the peony's sweet scent, the June heat,
the shiny mica in the gravel
ground into her under-flesh,
and the damp clumps
of last year's leaves I settled over her,
before I carried her off to a mossy softer place
as if I could make amends in those hours
when I knelt and let her see. *Sister,*
I said. *I did it. It was me.*

Christmas Eve Afternoon at Braddock Bay

Rennie McQuilkin

for Eleanor and Will

And it was said that we should go to see this thing
come to us from afar. So we set forth over fields
simplified by snow and ice, bent low to negotiate
an avenue of wild rose arched by weight of winter,
its red *hips* ripe; passed a stand of cattails,
umber seed-tubes broken into beige wool redolent
as spice; and came to an endless lake, steel-blue under
a lowering anthracite sky ornamented by salmon trim
at its distant edge. Along the shore past bare willows
glowing from within, a serration of waves broke, all
but frozen. From the rock-ridden jut of a long spit
hung teeth of ice—a place as austere

as the cold cattle shed and tooth-gnawed slats of a
small corn crib we'd hallow as a manger that night,
nursery of God. Here, now, at the heart of wilderness
was the mystery we'd come far to see, at first nothing:
a white-topped, white-and-gray-striped boulder
at the far end of the promontory. Then the white top
of the boulder moved, swiveled like a lighthouse
illuminating a circle of the world, searching into us:
the oval, gold-eyed face of a Snowy Owl
from the Arctic tundra, a creature so fiercely itself
it was the proof I was looking for.

Praise Song

Rennie McQuilkin

> *The nocturnal African dung beetle is the only known*
> *non-vertebrate to navigate and orient itself by the Milky Way*

Now let us praise Dung Beetles who
roll balls of excrement towering
over them. Faced with such an ordeal,
Sisyphus might have called it quits.
But these leggy, body-armored fellows
sculpt, roll, and stash away fecal stuff
250 times their own weight nightly
for progeny born in the bosom of dung.

See them clamber to the top
of their globes and orient themselves
by the stars, dead-reckoning
like ancient Polynesians
at home in their wilderness of ocean.

Whale Watching, Scammon's Lagoon, Baja
Elizabeth Kudlacz

> *The narrow, rural Carretera Transpeninsular Highway runs over 1,000*
> *miles, stretching from Tijuana to Cabo San Lucas.*

There's only one road, coyote lean and novena long. Road
of boojum. Road of cardon. Of holy cholla and pink blooms
pinned to pinch like small acts of contrition.

Road of gringos. Road of narcos. Then no one
for miles except shamans splayed in ochre
across dim walls of distant caves.

Road of lost goat. Road of dead dog and vulture
perched between barb and thorn. Road of night,
fused with sky so star-filled I searched

for any ember along the road of day,
beneath sky heavy with orange of gravid trees
and blue of the panga tipping leeward as if

to lose pilgrims to lagoon. Twelve pairs
of hands reaching out to fluke, to fin. To finger
the holy rosary of its spine rising in slow arc.

The photo I did not take: its great breath
breaking the calm. My baptism
in its blow.

A Poem for the Poet Hermithrush, Who Gave Me, Shi Lu, a Cricket Cage

Stanford M. Forrester

I still can't catch
the cricket that sings
every night
on my back porch

I just want to hear
a few songs
to soothe away
my loneliness

while looking for him
I only found a toad
but his voice
was too deep

and he was
too fat anyway
to fit
into the cage

as acorns fall
& autumn
soon
to end

I fear I'll have to spend
all these
days & nights
singing to myself

Fox, December Snow

Louis Gabordi

A limping fox is hunting on the hill below the cliffs
on a morning made more lovely by an early winter snow.
She moves two legs and hops across the white.
Her head is cocked and low as she listens for the mice
that scratch and gather on the hidden ground.
I have seen her hunting many times, switching back
along the slope and pausing at the piles of brush
I leave for warmth and cover every autumn.
Her arrival after dawn should be less surprising,
less remarkable by now, but fur the color of wood fire
is always unexpected. I want to think she'll heal before
her hunger and the cold can do her in.

What happens to a fox? I hear the fisher screaming
like a child from time to time. And a bobcat hunts
these woods again and will not tolerate a fox.
Can a dying vole inflict a wound that festers?
Or was it something tamer, a hidden stem of thorns?
Do even foxes slip on icy rocks and turn an ankle?

The natural world is pushing me again to challenge
my assumptions, to reconsider who and what I am.
Am I a man who would, if she'd allow it,
wrap her in a tattered towel and lay her in a basket?
There is a place not far from here where people
know about these things and understand
what mercy is for injured foxes.

If I found her lying on her side,
saw her rib cage pulsing through her fur,
could I ignore the fear that rose with every step
as I approached? Could I endure the fetid air
of animal necrosis, control my thoughts and hands
to give her what I think she needs? Or is my compassion
better left untested, and merely what a well-fed man
can summon in a heated room?

Nothing is resolved before she finishes,
decides there's nothing here for her
and struggles up the hill into the beech and maples.
As she moves along the naked saplings by the stony ledge,
stripes of shadow and the sifted copper sun
obscure and then reveal her. When she pauses
I can see no sign of weakness, only an undiminished
fox's wild beauty. She waits as though she understands.
Her stillness at a distance is itself an act of kindness,
warm, flowing down the hill and pooling at my feet.

One

Pit Pinegar

A young lizard thrashes in water,
then stops. By the time I get to him,
he's still, floating on his back, dead,
it appears; army green, black,
gray—an intricacy of stripes and
yellow dots, impossible to see
until he's right-side-up, unmoving,
in my palm. *You don't have to die,*
I say, as though I can coax him back
over a threshold. After a long while,
his tail twitches. I stroke his tiny body,
no thicker than a pencil. I imagine
each stroke draws oxygen in. After
an even longer while, his body
convulses. Still again. I lay him in shade—
out of the 100-degree Tucson afternoon
watch. At twenty minutes, he lifts
his head, ten minutes later, his tail.
I glance away…and back. Gone. I have
spent forty minutes talking to
a lizard as though the vibration of
my voice could trigger a response
in him that might pass for breathing.
There was nobody to see or hear
the limitlessness of my attention,
the chiding of my own subversive
voice: *It's just a lizard for goodness
sake.* And the other voice: *But I am
here. I saw a thrashing creature
go still.* And for a time that lizard
is *the* most beautiful and necessary
sentient I've ever beheld. Not to
intervene would mark me. For less
than an hour, lizard and I are no
longer he and I, no longer imperiled
and rescuer, no longer separate;
I am water-logged, without breath,

then I am resting, resting in the shade
in a fierce landscape, *one* until
he re-enters his skin and disappears.

Snapshot: Four Turkeys at the Feeder

Daniel Donaghy

Second day of spring, I woke
to four wild turkeys gobbling on
cracked shells below our feeders.
They brought no chaos to the morning:
bright blue over the mountains,
wrens picking suet as they always do
and flying off, finches pulling thistle
through socks, cardinals swooping
back and forth for sunflower seeds.

Each turkey a good twelve pounds
and almost tall as my waist,
same height as my daughter, who's five,
who'd love to see this after school:
animals from her *Little House* books
feasting right here in our yard.

Another of her books taught us
turkeys can fly fifty miles an hour,
glide thousands of feet without flapping,
scratch through six inches of ice
to lift scraps of midwinter food.
All instinct and shifts through resistance.
All blood ritual and desire,

their eyes are three times better than ours,
can spot slight movements from a hundred yards.
Their gobbles travel a quarter of a mile.

These turkeys, though, are for the moment
plain as pigeons, or plain as any of us
who have wandered far off course
and want only enough of a meal
to keep going toward what we know.
They eat slowly and don't fuss.
They don't strut their feathers
or drag their wings on the ground.
They don't scare the squirrel

or woodpecker or red-winged blackbirds.
They lean into one another.
They pay no attention to me at the window,
zooming in, zooming out,
shooting only photos, again and again.

Encroachment

Tom Nicotera

How have the creatures through the years
adapted to us?
They no longer run but encroach:
bear, coyote, bobcat, moose,
deer, opossum, raccoon, skunk,
the elusive fisher, the rumored cougar.
How do they identify us?
By the flashing eyes of our cars,
the skin so hard only falling acorns dent it,
the frightening noise that comes and goes
with our spinning feet?
What horrors of tooth and fang
must they imagine come
from such a roaring mouth?
They've probably learned to fear
the rushing crush of our weight
as we strike down road crossers without warning.
What other bits of terrifying knowledge
have been passed through the generations?
When do they know to run? To hide?
To invade our yards, raiding
our birdfeeders, our gardens, our garbage?
When do they know to harvest our pets?
When will we know what they know?

The Song of the Dusky Seaside Sparrow
Clare Rossini

trebles through   my tinny speakers
hauled in   by a click of the mouse

from an archive   at Cornell
A sound so clear   I can almost see the bird

perched on a curl   of spartina grass
its body   flecked with black   an extravagant

streak of yellow   brow-ing each eye
Does it call to its mate?

Or to chicks in the nest   mouthing air?
Some scientists say   the Dusky sang simply

for the sake of it
another sound   raised to counter   the waves'

polished grind   and bleak withdrawals
How is it   that the species that designs

sparrow-cides   and sites freeways
through nesting grounds   also salvages

so that with   a finger's pressure
on an acquiescent key   I can make an extinct

bird sing?
I crank up my laptop's volume   click the link

There—
a husky   spiel of notes

From the dogwood   at my window
a local sparrow answers   with sturdy chirrup

Again, the Dusky's   purled trill
the duet   going on

The Museum of the Forever Gone

Edwina Trentham

Here to the left, is the room of small things, the few
we had time to gather. Although, in truth, almost
everything you will see here is small. This flower,
a violet, once carpeted the ground purple,
and next to it, notice that cluster of perfect
little blossoms, how they form a circle of Queen
Anne's Lace, which once caught the sun from its long green stalks,
white heads humming with bees. We have one
example of a bee here, but sadly the tack
has damaged the soft fuzz of its back. Still, beside
the bee is a butterfly, again only one,
but it's a Monarch, and worth seeing, with its gold
and black stained-glass spread of wings. Let's move on now. Turn
right to check out our fish and our amphibians.

Yes, just a few fish and none very big, but note
the silvery overlap of their scales. And next
to them, our frogs. We have two if you count the toad.
We almost missed them because we were not paying
close attention to the rush of their vanishing.
But look over here at the snake with a frog half-
way down its throat, just two green legs showing. Ah, snakes,
they slithered and coiled everywhere once, some thicker
than your arm, some finger-thin. But again, we have
only this one black snake on display. Still, what luck
to find a snake swallowing a frog, to pin up
on the wall as one! Here is our small bird corner.
The larger birds, eagles and hawks, are depicted
downstairs in the mural you'll pass on your way out.

But first, lean close to this tiny hummingbird's once
emerald wings, now faded to gray, and, sad to say
its long bill was torn off when whoever found it
crammed it into his pocket. But we have a tit-mouse
and a chickadee, bright-eyed, common, and countless.
For some reason, we have pinned a bat skeleton
among the birds, although bats were mammals like us.
Still, note the way the bat has been displayed, to show

how like a human its body was, arms spread wide
to show the delicate membranes of both its wings,
its legs akimbo. I heard that bats spoke to each
other in full sentences, but that could be myth.
No one to ask now. Ah, here is a fine transition right
into insects, the primary food source for bats.

We have only a minute selection of what
were millions of these six-legged creatures. You must
strain to see, but I believe that might be a gnat.
Oh, those three in the bottom row, the ones with eight
legs, are really spiders. Well, that's all we have here,
so let's go downstairs, past the beautiful mural,
started by a woman who was still alive just
before there was nothing. She was very old, died
before she could complete her work, so as you see,
she painted mostly trees, because she wanted us
to imagine them, how their green branches feathered
the sky, before we murdered them, before they tore
up the earth with their dying. And though we can't hear
it—she painted birdsong, birdsong, endless birdsong.

The Trembling

John L. Stanizzi

> *Pando is a clonal colony of an individual male quaking aspen
> located in south-central Utah. It is a single living organism
> with a root system of 106 acres estimated to be 80,000 years old.*

Poplars, just like people, are trembling most
of the time; the poplars because of the
flatness and angle of their petioles
to the wind. That flatness causes tremors.
The trembling we see in people? Who knows?

Quaking aspen, *populus tremulous*,
contingent upon the wind to make them
quiver like tethered birds struggling to fly,
grove of lonely women, in love, trembling;
Hopkins writes, *"...if we but knew what we do..."*

Mona Lisa, violas, harp-poachers—
mere divertimenti against life's aches.
Let's talk about Pando and the clonal
colony of quaking aspens that have
quaked for 80,000 years, grace past art.

It's raining, coming down in hordes, and a
man, or is it a stone, sits at the base
of a tree. It's a man and he's trembling.
Colonies of poplars, natural shrines
tremble, too, and the moon weeps light through rain.

Imagine if, like the poplars, we all
shared the same DNA; how we'd all quake
and shimmer, even changing our colors.
How the world would tremble with this sameness,
sacrificing our leaves to the bare wind.

Poplars, just like people, are trembling, most
contingent upon the wind to make them.
Let's talk about Pando and the clonal
colonies of poplars, natural shrines
sacrificing their leaves to the bare wind.

Old Souls

Jeanne LeVasseur

after Mary Oliver

Do trees think?
Are there sparks in their neural network underground?
Who made them so—the dogwood, and the maple?
Who made the shadblow,
the June-blooming, dainty-white one,
that ropes along the river when fish run their spawning marathon?
Who made the speckled alder,
and gave it woolen cones to hang like lanterns
through the winter? Who knit the hickory its shaggy bark
or pieced the sycamore its quilt of buff and tan?
And I have not spoken of the oak, with its shapely limbs
and apronful of acorns, its waxy leaves
full as dinnerplates for the swallows.
Or mentioned the quaking aspen shaking her petticoats
of tufted cotton in the breeze.
They make me wonder—do trees have souls?
I feel a hollow place in my chest open like a nest.
If the soul begins with longing,
then these roots that twine in tributaries
underground or the call that ruffles a canopy of leaves—
this is how it starts, this longing to join
one soul to another.

Silver Birch

Katherine Szpekman

> *In Sanskrit, birch bark is bhurga,*
> *a tree whose bark is used to write upon.*

The pupil held me in an unsettling stare.
Thin black lines etched the body and face.
A reptilian eye, an amulet or nazar,
rimmed in black kohl.
A serpent ready to strike.

I pulled the dog back.
A scroll of birch bark rested
in damp grass and earth,
curled in a silver patina.

I stooped to pick up this offering,
carried home this symbol of love,
new beginnings and protection,
and nestled it among my books.

It is too late to place it in my babies' cradles,
to ward off evil, to add it to a kettle
to cast protection spells,
to make brooms to sweep out the old,
cleanse the past.

But it is not too late to write poems
upon each peeling twirl,
to join the sway and arch,
the flutter of heart-shaped leaves,
as wind lifts
and disperses words like seeds.

It is not too late to listen to the birch sing.
Our voices,
their salve and fire,
soothing and incendiary.

Ashford Oak

Denise Abercrombie

Praise the spider at the center of her web
standing vigil in your shadow.
Praise your lightning scars & splits, see-through twists,
the rotting pulp of your boughs. Praise to the impossible
lift: tonnage of your hollowed-out heartwood.
To leaves that sprout & cling in spite of
gypsy moths, honey fungus & winds, praise.
Praise to stewards who protected & pruned, arborists
with their cables, sprays & feed, loggers & farmers who found
you too gnarled or sprawling to fell. Praise bare branches,
dark-ridged bark overgrown with trumpet vine
& praise your fallen crown.
Let poison ivy & briers overtake your many rings,
let raspberries ripen near your sunlit roots.
Praise to surrendering this sanctuary to brambles.
Praise this final bit of shade.

The Takedown

Joan Hofmann

I watched giants felled one
After another and another and…
The clearing took hours.
For hours I watched in horror
An efficiency of decimation.

In a single day the lot next to me
Transformed from an assurance
Of green-frilled broad canopy—
Sustained by sixty-foot-high trunks,
A beauty of curved barked stalks—
Into a cleared space.

The maples now gone, an until-now
Unseen interior is exposed: is this
Awkward gawking addictive
Or just inherited? Stunned, I am both
Curious and crestfallen.

I'm not the only one disoriented.

Like fingernails of dirt,
Some things you just can't forget.
The chewchewchew of the cardinal
The silhouette of the maples at daybreak
The mating pileated woodpeckers
The hoot-hoot-hoot of the lone owl.

The bone-chill noise of the chainsaw
The split, crack and thud of the drops
The stories' high pile of brush
(Brush? Such a light word for huge
Limbs that shook earth today.)
The scream-ring of the chipper, grinding.

Everyone's nest has been upended.
In the silence of emptiness
Under spareness of a too-blue sky

A scatter of sparrows arrives, one bird
After another, to make a necklace
On top of the new chain link fence:
Each stands facing the same direction
Toward the now barren
Space of the uprooted, the missing.

Bedtime Story

Edwina Trentham

There once were these beautiful things called trees.
Their branches—in greens you cannot dream
or imagine—feathered the sky, at times
still, then hushing, rustling, caught by a breeze,
leaves turning red, gold, brown, before they fell,
then glowing pink along a tracery
of black in spring, which used to come between
the hollow, white darkness we call winter
and summer's wildfires. But we wanted
more, then more, of everything, so they dried
to dust, gave up on us deep in their cores,
thundered to the earth, tearing up the dead
tangles of their massive roots. Sleep, now, sleep.
Tomorrow I will tell you about bees.

Of Stones and Time

Gwen Gunn

"I see my husband's stone wall still remains,"
the woman walking by stopped to say.
"Built it sixty years ago. Now passed.

I'm Italian, but I like black people."
"It certainly is a sturdy wall," I answered,
avoiding my black husband's laughing eyes.

Now it has stood over a hundred years,
although near driveway top we've knocked it wider,
and pranksters sometimes shove rocks aside.

Early on we had more stone walls built.
That young builder's nearly sixty now,
a geologist, so still he studies rocks.

His looks have changed, the wall is much the same.
Though just a year ago a stone worked free
in his six-foot wall behind a pull-off.

The rocks nearby were also coming loose.
I heaved them back in place, made sure
this wall will last past me.

Our story's short, that of these stones is long.
Rocks brought along from far north in a glacier,
were dropped here as the ice retreated.

In case we don't survive this sixth extinction,
stone pyramids, cathedrals, walls will stay
layered in the earth's crust to say:

"Those sapiens could build."

Stone Harvest

Ginny Lowe Connors

1.
Fields return to forest. Years ago the farmers left,
but stone walls remember them. Miles of walls in disrepair.
What a crop of stones those farmers had! I doubt they found
beauty in them, just more hard labor. But I admire
the tumbled walls meandering in autumn's sun and shadow.
History's here among a clutter of leaves, curling vines
and fallen logs. Islands of pale lichen bloom on the stones'
rough surfaces, and soft green moss invites my touch.

2.
New England Potatoes, they called them, Satan's Seeds—
the harvest of stones heaved up by frost, by roots,
by burrowing critters each year in fields once cleared.
Another endless chore to toss them to the edges of fields.
Or pile rocks on a stone sled, let the oxen pull. Heaps of stone
turned into boundary walls, packed together
with uprooted stumps and wooden rails. Built and rebuilt
with increasing care. Men laid stones one-on-two
or two-on-one, like brickwork, capped with flat fieldstones.
Sheep high, bull strong, hog tight.

3.
The rocks are flecked with mica, mineral-streaked
with rivulets dark or light. They keep company with bindweed,
bits of wood, seeds and leaves. Rest amid ferns and pokeweed.
A few are blackened, stained perhaps by campfires centuries ago,
when bands of people roamed these woods, but had no need
for walls. Unplowed, the topsoil then was so thick with humus,
most stones stayed buried. Secrets in the soil.

4.
When I rest my palms against a rock, I feel the heat
it's holding. But these stones hold memory of glaciers,
huge ice sheets that scraped the earth and carved
out slabs of bedrock. The ice retreated slowly,
dropping stones along the way.

5.

Storm-tossed trees have fallen on the walls. Roots and vines
nudge them apart. Seeds fall into crevices, hidden there
by chipmunks, mice, squirrels. Young trees take root
and grow between the rocks, squeezing them apart.
The new must push against the old, and storms
take some of us down. The plot of every history.
But remnants of wall are still here, weathered
and leached, eroded and stained, the stones
marvelous in their variety, their stubborn persistence.

6.

I touch a mossy stone tumbled near the dirt road
where I'm walking. Finger its scratches and stains.
My skin carries its own share of creases, marks and scars
after so many years of living, loving, working.
What more can I ask but that I've been of some use
before it's my turn to fall away and settle into
whatever may come next?

Nothing is Still in this World

Elaine Zimmerman

The startled rabbit sits in the yard.
White tailed; not too large or small.
Just the whiskers moving. Nothing else
is still. Bodies washed up in Fukushima.
Eyes big as fish before gutting.
Not three or four, but hundreds, like
sea kelp or shells lining the shore.

Still clothed, so many arms and legs jangled
and splayed. No fast footing quick enough
to beat the fierceness. The waves higher than
the market or narrow paths that climb
the village. Flailing bodies reaching for air
and answer. The world's undone in a single
breath and we all come shuddering down.

Hands on cheeks, open mouthed. Some hold
special objects, a stone or coin. The last act
before a tremor. Then everything washed away.
Each gesture and sound quieted now. No speech
to speak of but an endless stun in the eye
as if the world turned upside down on those
remaining, just before the heaving sounds.

Toddlers plant tea seedlings in rice fields,
six each, to touch green-stemmed growth.
But even the simple cow, icon of field and farm,
is a menace now. All milk pulled from market.
Wild parsley contaminated in Singapore.
The humble turnip, tainted. Radiation arrives
in northern California, like an upended whale.

Rooftops and tires floating. Masked toddlers
line up for iodine. It is cold, so cold. Truly,
nothing is still in this world. Even the chair,
empty as poor luck, goes back and forth.

No one in it but fierce winds. The sky gray
as dreams before they fly away. Only
the rabbit stares, waiting like a still life.

Jump,   Jive,   and Whale

Joanie DiMartino

*"While you take in hand to school others, and to teach them by what
name a whale-fish is to be called in our tongue, leaving out, through
ignorance, the letter H, which almost alone maketh up the signification
of the word, you deliver that which is not true."*
—Richard Hakluyt the Younger

On the surface, a churn of white foam: salted,   ripened,

where the slick hump of whale   slips   singing
into depths,   undetected by our barque's night watch,

though below in the hold,   the casked oil
quavers   as if haunted   with this forlorn
      nocturne   of leviathans.

In the foc's'le, another kind of salt,   the tattoo-muscled sweat
from the heated pitch   of a watch off duty:

     banjo player,   skinny bonesman,
pulsing breath of harmonica   then   the booming bass
        fills the space

that exhilarates   us exhausted whalers
into rousing stomp   and jounce   while our feet sail
off sea chests   and we spin   to the strum
     and the drum
   both   the bold   and the brute.

We perceive these beasts through the intimacy   of slaughter,

bloodied blowholes   and cutting in,
   boats stove to splinters   in the twisted beauty
of a frothing   breach ~

yet there is kinship   among males   who make   loneliness
    sonorous   in this souse of silken brine,

so when asked why we don't   hunt humpbacks,
     we will say   the humpbacks sink,   instead of say

the humpbacks   sing.

Sea Smoke

James Finnegan

From the shore it looks like the whole world is burning.
That odd phenomenon after a cold snap, a smoky fog
rising off the waters as far as one can see. I can't see
as far as I once could. But I do see and hear the news.

Someone spotted a snowy owl behind the beach parking lot,
posted a picture of it perched atop a Do Not Enter sign.
I know what Jeffers would say: Let it burn, let the people
be stewed, swallowed up by the burning seas. So be it.

A little too forgiving, with far too much hope, walking back
to the car, I pick up someone's fast-food cup, try to shove it
down the maw of an overflowing trashcan that no one
is getting paid to empty. When Gandhi was asked what he

thought of Western civilization, he replied, "I'm in favor of it."
The sun setting in the west turns the eastern sky pink,
and I'd like to say the effect made everything more beautiful.
No, the sea smoke was now backlit as by fire. The ancients
made offerings to fire. We offend by making fire our offering.

At the End of Empire

Mary Guitar

1. Falling

Looking out across the horizon
I imagine the American Empire itself
enfolded in that stately
snarl of purple clouds
sailing toward me
about to crash
into sheer rockface. Here
the air glows, granite boulders
pulse with a meaning
that words no longer contain.

The wind smells of rain falling on dry soil
and ozone, silvery and sharp.
And then it is upon us: air no longer air but water,
colors streaming, peonies melting, foxgloves bowing, roses
pressing their drenched faces against the trellis.

Lightning reveals all things in negative,
every card reversed, one bright flash dealt out,
then another, then wind moves through dark trees.
Take that, or that, or—
leave it.

2. Rising

Last night in a crowded dream
I looked out across a long green field.
The sky, sooty yellow, darkened into twilight.
Something waited. As we watched—five, ten, one hundred
immense glowing sky lanterns slowly rose, drifted upward
buoyed by the flaming candles tucked inside,
great loops of rope suspended below them. On each rope
a young monk stood, silently holding on.
Sometimes two balanced together, touching shoulders.
Heads shaved, saffron robes flowing, they faced forward
and resolutely squared their shoulders.

We couldn't see their faces but knew they were not afraid.
We watched and the animals watched
until their lights were as small as stars.
Then we prepared
to follow.

3. Fleeting

What we know of the world could be balanced on
the carapace of this beetle with the pink face stripes;
on the stately dowager beauty of the faded wild columbine,
upright but deconstructing; and on the lazy questions and answers
of birds at twilight. The obedient grass
bows over paths we've beaten to reach this place
where the air still smells of honeysuckle and water and truth.
Safety nests under the brambles but nowhere else.

Here, we must know the predators: their beauty, their disguises,
the deep reach of their sight and hearing, and know
that some of us will die in their mouths. This moon,
this scrap of eyelash caught in bare branches,
is tonight the only thing that lifts our hearts. Once freed
from the tree-tops, it chases the stars, those hieroglyphs hinting
at the nature of life behind the scrim—
transient glances, fugitive color, like the signal lights
of great ships or the green flash of fireflies
pulsing in an unknown code.

4. Grieving

The pain sinks deep into muscles
strained on the rough trek into the rocky cavern
we did not know we contained
and have not mapped. Some of us are confused,
some outraged. Some insist that life is still spinning
in a pure and predetermined orbit.
If we could hold our grief in our arms like a newborn
would we see its other face—our love for the world?
When grief rises behind my tongue, into my throat,
I open my mouth and utter words
in a language I have never studied.
The void offers up genus and species,

the flavors of the world roll under the tongue.
Sweet, sharp, salty, pungent, piercing,
they pulse in our pleasure centers
until we are sated.

The little blue *Schizachyrium scoparium*
stings my calves as I pick early berries
while the secret names tumble off my tongue
so that they may live in the air a little longer:
buteo jamaicensis, red-tailed hawk dipping and circling.
The caterpillar *Orgyia leucostigma*.
so voracious, so toxic, so beautiful,
may be erased if I do not say its name
with appropriate solemnity. Or even if I do.

5. And What Follows

In the garden, green beans
still punctuate the trellis with hopeful commas,
and at the edge of the cornfield
the sun's last eloquent lance
burnishes the black raspberries.
Listen, the rusting engines
that lie in the ground below us
flash like distant heat lightning,
like fireflies, like code. Listen,
I think we must unfold our grief
and find the sharp shard wrapped inside
the bundle.

6. And Again

Beside us, the elders carve sweeping lines into rock
with the sharp shards of our grief, incise flowing shapes
that remind us of peaceful mornings, of evenings
when there is plenty, keeping untouched
what is carved there already, and the empty wall
around the corner.

A Brief History of Everything

Pat Hale

Rain.

> Rain fell for a long time, and then it stopped.
> Rain fell until the ground was washed away,
> and us with it. Then the bird came.

Flight.

> We all could fly, and speak the simple language of birds.
> *This is important,* the bird said, *remember this.*
> A sharpness to that beak against the ear.

Feathers.

> Another storm, another night, another sea
> of churning clouds. *Hold on,* the bird said,
> and then there were wings reaching out to us.

Advice.

> *Let go,* the bird said, and we did, but we were afraid,
> and still the rain kept falling and us again with it,
> into the canyon, down to where the river flowed.

Recovery.

> When the storm stopped, the river ran clear.
> The sun came out. We were amazed.
> *Of course,* the bird said, *the sun always comes back.*

Separation.

> Birds in the air, birds in the cliffs, all watching
> as we tried to remember the language they'd taught us.
> It came back, but only to some, and they flew away.

Exile.

The rest of us remained behind, earthbound
with our heavy feet. Unvoiced, scrabbling in the mud,
we made symbols with our sticks and called them words.

Acqua Alta

Laura Mazza-Dixon

When Venice floods, as it has for centuries,
the waters of the Adriatic Sea cross the piazza
and climb the steps of the basilica like pilgrims.

The rest of us pull on our boots and cross
on narrow wooden walkways, waiting in pairs
to enter the ancient bronze portals of San Marco.

A sacred darkness lies within, a world broken,
gleaming in tiny squares of gold, glass and stone,
mosaics of the stories of a world being made.

>At the top of a cupola, God reaches
>toward a dark orb. Wide rays of light
>stream from a red sun and a grey moon.

>A dove flies above the watery depths.
>Land appears. Plants and trees begin to grow.
>When birds fill the sky, fishes fill the water.

>Pairs of dromedaries, lions, leopards,
>striped boar and elephants appear
>beneath God's outstretched hand.

Venice has lasted many centuries at sea level, resting
on wooden poles driven so deep into the airless clay
beneath the water that they are immoveable, petrified.

In the lagoon, crabs and shrimp, octopus and squid,
sea bass and anemones thrive in the marsh
where tidal currents meet freshwater rivers.

Gulls and cormorants gather by the fishing boats.
Herons perch on the *bricole* that mark the channels
where ships once carried silks and spices back from Egypt.

>In the cupola, the figure of Adam is molded
>from dark material by God himself, and led

through a door into a verdant garden.

After he names the gathered animals, Adam lays
his hand on the lion's head. Then he falls asleep
under a tree to wake with Eve beside him.

All is well until they decide not to listen to God.
God escorts them back out the door
into a dry place where nothing can grow.

In the Old Testament, no matter how many prophets
cried out against the greed and wickedness on earth
no-one seemed to pay any attention.

No-one but Noah, who walked with God and listened
to his growing frustration with the selfishness
and corruption of those he had created with such care.

God is so angry he has determined to destroy
every living thing on earth with a flood,
and tells Noah exactly how to build an ark.

Lately, the *acqua alta* visits Venice more often,
sweeping over the islands that protect the lagoon,
climbing further up the steps of the basilica.

Last November, the moon rose over the city
when the tides were running high,
the lagoon full of rain from an earlier storm.

The Sirocco, a wind that originates in Egypt
and blows across the Adriatic from the south,
was strengthened by unusually warm air.

In less than an hour, the winds drove water
from the lagoon into the Piazza San Marco,
flooding it to a depth of nearly two meters.

Waves pounded up and over the steps of the basilica,
through the Byzantine portals, and into the atrium,
just beneath the mosaics of Noah and the Flood.

Salt water filled the sanctuary, damaging the geometric
stonework of the marble floors, weakening pillars
and submerging tombs in the crypt below.

Noah builds a door in the hull of the ark,
begins to gather the pairs of birds and animals
God has instructed him to save.

Surrounded by pairs of red-legged partridges,
ring-necked pheasants, moorhens and mallards,
four guinea hens and seven white geese,

he lifts a peacock and a peahen in his arms
and prepares to put them into the ark
while the pelicans and herons wait in line.

Pairs of leopards, goats and antelope
stand watching while he guides a lioness,
symbol of San Marco, into the door in the hull.

God waits for Noah's family to climb aboard
and closes the small door from the outside
just as the floodgates of the deep burst open.

In the next mosaic, only the heads and shoulders
of the people floating in the water are visible,
a wall of wavy dark water above and behind them.

The *acqua alta* no longer arrives in Venice
as pilgrims would, but as a conquering army
from a far-off land, all force and no mercy.

To watch the footage of the rushing tide is to sense
the fear the Venetians must have felt as the water
rose higher and higher around them in the darkness.

When the waters of the Adriatic Sea reach the mosaics
that illuminate the darkness of that sanctuary,
the world as we know it will have ended too.

Water Water

Julia Paul

Lather of ocean, twist of river. Dirty dishwater.
Water, daughter, cup and saucer. Boiling kettle.
Steam whistle. Cup to parched lips
of the homeless, of the refugee. Cup to parched lips
of the desert, of the creek bed. Rain brailling sand
and mud. Rain writing on rooftops. On many tongues—
water, agua, vatten, wasser, voda, vand.

Ashes scattered over waves: brother, mother, lover.
Weight of water pressing down. On the brink of rain.
On the brink of tears. Like holding water in the palms
of one's hands. Washing hands for two minutes,
for one *Hail Mary*, one *Happy Birthday*. Songs sung
by the water: hum, drum and simmer. Wings skimming
water. Light skimming water. Light dancing on water.
Water-fire. Fire-water. Drench, drown, drunk.

Reflection in a pond. In bubbles from a wand. Black, blue,
silver water under the moon and stars water. Puddle-stained
lane. Rainbow oil slick. Body hitting water. Jumping
from a bridge, rocks in the pocket water. Water under the bridge.
Wishes in the well-water. Filtered, fluoridated, flushed water.

Chemical waste water. Carbonated, chlorinated, distilled water.
Funneled, poured and puddled water. Water from the faucet.
Water for chocolate, for crops. Drip drop water. Born of water.
Thirst storming. Warming waters. Source, shortage, torture,
slaughter for water. Cistern, aqueduct, tongue, gullet.
Melting waters. Rising tides. In over your head water.

Seaplane

Charles Rafferty

The seaplane circles the lake, checking for logs and swimmers. It is a further confirmation that we want to go everywhere, unconstrained, like the smell of dead skunk on Sugar Street. Columbus didn't care if his inadvertent genocide came to define him. He was looking for pepper and cinnamon. The unaimed bullet goes on with its exploration. The avalanche speeds toward level ground.

Rock Me Mama

Christie Max Williams

1.

O Mama, rock me.
Rock me in the arms of your sex,
your birth, your wild plenty.

Rock me your full moon in May,
rock me horseshoe crabs by the millions
on the beaches of Delaware Bay,
let me see the moonlight on their ancient armor
as they pave the beach like countless cobbles,
as the great she-crabs pull trains
of he-crabs coupled to their engines
in urgent readiness to spawn the eggs
she'll lay by thousands in the wet dark sand.

Rock me the break of day
when blizzards of shorebirds shift and juke as one
in crazy flight above the crabs,
sing me their names—
red knots, plovers, sanderlings, and turnstones—
sing the epic journey that brings them
from Tierra del Fuego bound for Arctic nesting grounds,
sing hunger, sing exhaustion, as they descend
upon the bowls of crab eggs on the beach,
gorging themselves on the glistening fecundity,
then rising into flight with peeping cries,
as they've done for a thousand thousand full moons in May!
O Mama, can it last?
Can crabs and birds endure
The rising sea, the shrinking shore?

We owe you a tender cooling, Mama—
we owe you a cooling.

2.

Rock me, Mama.
Rock me in the lap of your tidal sway,
your ebb and surge, your procreant surge.

Rock me a long Alaskan summer day
when salmon schooling by the millions—
Chinook, Coho, Sockeye, Pink—
surge from the sea where the years
have grown them into mighty swimming muscles
flexing with fertility,
surging to shore in search of natal waters,
every brook, stream, and river
a salmon birthplace and destiny
where they will spawn and die.

Rock me the secret salmon compass
pointing unfailingly to home,
as the silent silver salmon
fly swiftly through the water,
then break the surface into air-born flight,
slicing the horizon in flexing flight,
a salmon exultation of grace, fertility, and fate,
as they have done for a thousand thousand summers!
Ah Mama, can it last?
Will the salmon's compass point through warmer waters?
Will shrinking glaciers feed their natal streams?

A tender cooling, Mama—
You are owed a cooling.

3.

O rock me, rock me, Mama.
Rock me with your cooing call,
your lullaby of screech and howl,
your deep deep quiet.

Rock me a starry sky in early March,
rock me silence of the frozen banks
along the Platte River in Nebraska,

let me peer through darkness
at the starlit river, the wide slow Platte,
its silent shallow current skimming over ancient mud,
as the horizon silvers with approaching dawn.
Let me almost see the slender silhouettes,
let me in the sky's faint first pink
see ten thousand silhouettes
of sandhill cranes standing in the shallows,
and let me hear a soft first chortle
as a lone crane rises into wide-winged flight,
as suddenly a thousand cranes rise as one,
and a thousand more, ten thousand more,
lifting into flight against the pinkening sky,
their collective wings a sudden woosh,
their collective chortle a mighty cry
as the sky becomes a cloud of cranes,
tens of thousands wheeling a wide wild circle,
crying a deafening cry of crane-ness,
as they have cried for a thousand thousand dawns in March.
Dear Mama, can it last?
Will the Platte's wide shallows dry to silt?
Will the cranes find haven here before
they leave to nest in Arctic Canada?

O Mama, a cooling, a tender cooling.

One Point Five Degrees Celsius

Carol Chaput

*The impacts of climate change are being observed earlier in the Arctic,
and with more immediate and severe consequences. The Arctic is warming
at a rate almost twice the global average.*
—Marine Mammal Commission

Wherever you are and wherever I am,
we need an antidote for the despair of degrees.
   Let us stop, walk out into the boreal mystery until the sacred reveals itself.
   Let us attend to the stars under the vault of the night sky and
learn this landscape, its scent and subtleties, its day and night.
   Let us stand in the brilliance of sheets of shining ice, in halos of spray until
we remember the memories of its fields, the low-growing arctic willows
over long-buried bones, a bowhead's rib.

Note the arctic fox trotting
over snow fields, leaving no prints—he stops,
hunkers down, nose tapping the wind,
searching for scents.

Witness the gray wolf toeing
delicately across the loosening tundra—he stops,
licks the milk-blue lichens
clenched to red rockfaces.

Heed the herd of reindeer drifting
like frost smoke and know when they
stop, still as stones, they see ahead
around the curve of time.

   Let us walk through snow over glistening threads of wild grasses
under frozen fields and let our minds and memory shape the land
We can learn to live wisely, and well.

For this moment, stand still in the icy air and—look—see the droplets
   of your breath fall frozen to the ground. The Arctic people call it the
whispering of stars.

Who Asks the Question?

Lana Orphanides

Who asks if the world is worth saving when
the light through the birch trembles and its leaves
play motets of whispering sound, surviving
these thirty years, through storms and storms and more
storms, floods and wind, and tide, and washed-up
boats against its side, and still it stands,
singing in its trebles of notes as it rises
above the house, its greenhearts of leaves,

its seeds like engines or flying birds
or angels who refuse to die, engendering
life, offering grace, each of us saying,
the tree and I, the world is worth saving.
The trees, the trees will show us how to speak
to one another, how to save the world.

How to Feed a Child

Catherine DeNunzio

Set on linen before the hungry child—
bleached starfish & bifurcated rock.

The five-fingered shell
is something fragile she can care for.

Porous enough to filter hurt,
reveal itself in light.

Intriguing enough to kindle desire.
Enough like bone to build on.

Enough like bone to say,
do not waste this life.

She will marvel at the rock—
its ivory left & ebony right—

and trace the russet vein between.
She will push her thumbs

into its hollows & curl her palm
around its knobby shoulder,

lift using both hands to gauge
its heft, her strength.

Swing her bare feet.
Wonder what tomorrow's feast will be.

Rare Grasses

Maria Sassi

> *monocotyledon: a class or subclass of herbaceous seedplants...*
> *parallel-veined leaves and floral organs...*

Oh, we have listened to the singing grass
the way the learned singer wrote
sermons in sun and soft rain—
whispered lores, promised healings
from palms near a river, woven cradle
for the found child.
                              Spreading earth
held the tangled roots. Blue
spangles grew on blades of green
and we rolled in them down hills of
Seton Park, whirling our sky around us...
now rarely seen. Once we believed
the opening to heaven was blue as the
flowering stars of the grass—our bodies
of light would rise on their scented waves.

Field Service

Christine Beck

In my teenage years,
instead of shopping at the mall,
I spent my Saturdays
selling leaflets door to door.

My mission was to announce
the coming war of Armageddon,
when everyone who wasn't saved
would face a fiery death.

We called it Field Service.
I recall those years one Sunday
in Vermont, as I embark
down a meandering country lane.

I find a field of green alfalfa. It grows
beneath a row of pines that seem to guard
the tender shoots like ministers or wise men.

Nearby an ancient graveyard lies locked
behind a picket fence, festooned
with Black-eyed Susans, the headstones
smoothed by weather and the years.

I rest beneath of the comfort of the trees,
breathe in the incense of the fields,
where no one knows if you are saved or damned.

Amid the harmony of growing things,
I plant my past beneath the earth
and sing the praise of pines.

Bats

D. Walsh Gilbert

Who will praise them? Who will praise
the woodland bats hanging
from the stand of trees on Talcott Mountain?
The soundless ones, the ones
who nurse their pups the size of thimbles,
who laud the dark,
the moonless nights and fog and rain,
who snatch and swallow
biting ticks and flying bugs,
and pollinate while sipping amber nectar.

Praise the mysterious,
the toothed ones, the skin-winged and eared
who hear what we cannot,
who cling to bending branches,
who shelter from weasel and snake
and roost slip-knotted to their colony.
Praise the Little Brown Bat,
the Pipistrelle, and Silver-Haired,
who navigate magnetic fields—
the warm-blooded ghosts who, upside-down,
locate the world.

Calling the Owl

Terry Bohnhorst Blackhawk

This time the owl eludes us
where we stand trying to call him in
                              with his own voice,
which we've captured on tape
to release to the predawn woods.

Press a button. The air flutters,
rushing from our black box
                    what is hidden from us—
wing-like quaverings—
                    soft bursts of song.

If light mutes him, shadows offer hope,
and we listen so intently into them
                              the snowy meadow
suddenly seems wider, brighter
with news from beyond its perimeter.

Don't lift, I almost pray,
                    don't disappear.
Day will break soon enough.
Let us hear your faint vibrato and absorb
what is invisible, wild and nearly gone.

Mist thickens the silence, promises
patience, echo, sound not sight.
I will let that fluty tremolo find,
                              fill me, give voice
to emptiness. I hold my breath to sustain
                    the long vowel of night.

Showering Qi

Lisa Meserole

at Firefly Preserve, New Canaan, CT

The sun has set and darkness showers us with light.
Once upon a time not from the moon or heavens,
but fireflies. Fifty thousand of them
heart-pulsing in the meadow, up in the trees,
a bedtime story we think is make-believe.
Our eyes in disbelief, so turfed in green,
still trusting the tale that eclipsed our sparks.
We've poisoned our glow bodies,
but the well night's story speaks for itself,
truth in a million strokes of desire
that twinkle in the eye everywhere more than stars.
Our dreaming spaces lit again
from where the earth still breathes.

Anthropocene Birthday

Sarah P. Strong

Gift of equations
the empty orchard blossoming with snow

Gift of a haunting
the shadows of the animals in smoke

Gift of a cinder
the stars leapt from the bottom of the well

Gift of scar tissue
the afterimage scored for us like notes

Gift of our silence
so gently the sea covers up our words

Gift of a fever
the smell of thunder breaking up the heat

Gift of a morning
the votive candles going out like breath

Gift of our footsteps
the leaves we saw caught in the hedge are birds

Two Bowls

Lorraine Riess

> *Instructed by the City Planner to stop excavation if any native artifacts*
> *or bones were found, the site engineer took the crane operator aside*
> *later to say, "If you find anything...anything at all, don't stop,*
> *keep digging. Otherwise we'll be hung up with an archeological dig*
> *for six months."*
> —In conversation with a Building Contractor, San Diego, 1986

On a flight south past the edge of L.A.
we pass over brown hills of the Poway Range.
I see a builder has seized one more mound,
beheading its peak to create a new plateau
while bulldozer tracks cut in a winding road,
ascending, circular, purposeful scores
scarring once sacred burial grounds.

Relics will be hidden along with utility lines
and should it rain the asphalt oils
will saturate a swale over unmarked bones.
Ocher clay furrows, sun dried
snakes curve to squeeze in more lots
for stucco homes and buzz cut lawns
that demand more water from a trickle
still called the Colorado River.

Not far down the road from a thriving casino
a Native American museum displays
an overturned, russet brown, unglazed bowl
with the same coiled grooves I'd seen from the air.
These carvings a harbinger of what was to come,
their world turned upside down.

Arrangements for the Endangered

Susan Kinsolving

What crematorium will inter Hine's emerald
dragonfly, pour those iridescent green ashes
into a clear glass urn? What mortuary will lay
the Jamaican boa to rest in a thin narrow

elongated coffin? Or set on tufted satin
the Sumatran rhino before installing him in
the rhinoceros mausoleum? What "cause of death"
euphemism will pass for losing the pink fairy

armadillo or the African wild ass? Where is
the priest to offer last rites to St. Vincent's
parrot or the rabbi to bury Koch's pitta?
What cortege can attend all twenty-three sea turtles,

eight different whales, fifteen extravagant pheasants?
Must eighteen monkeys fit into one simian crypt?
How to embalm all those butterflies? What eulogy
for the clawless Cameroon otter? Who will write

an obituary for the Alabama beach
mouse? Or offer the epitaphs for Bulmer's fruit bat,
the Tampico pearly mussel, Oahu tree snail,
every black jaguar, every last gorilla?

For Berta Cáceres

Jonathan Andersen

who led the struggle to save the Río Gualcarque, Honduras
March 4, 1971–March 3, 2016

I first learn of your life in the news of your death,
so by the time I discover *The Mother of All Rivers*, this brief
documentary like a deep bright pool, by the time I hear
your voice gliding over jump cuts (boulders rolling
and hopping down into the dusty roadblock, clouds
parting over dark green peaks like hands concealing, then
revealing a face); by the time I hear you explain *we denounced*
this dam and were threatened with smear campaigns,
imprisonment, and murder; by the time I see Tomás Garcia,
smiling in his white cowboy hat, move into slow-mo, then
his coffin bobbing between pallbearers; by the time the film ends
on the now agonizing high note of you, in profile, a strong
current churning past, you are dead. Who were the assassins?
What day could not be won by your wide-open face, open
eyes lit up like those of the girl you used to be?
You remind us that in the misty spray, in the cosmos
of your people, girls are never victims, will never be caught
running away or into the arms of soldiers: they guard
the quick-bending frothy uprush of Río Gualcarque—
without them, and in this life, not myth, without you,
the river would only tumble so far down from the mountains,
would never reach the boy standing at the outcrop poised
to dive, or the corn doing its whispery little dance
in the field, the steaming pot, the work clothes dunked
and wrung. In the film, you talk and gesture, march alongside
the pickup trucks, banners waving above fists and shouts
on the long road to the capital. Berta: I want to be
hidden in a shadow the night they broke into your home, burst
out to shoot them before they shoot you: I have never killed
anyone but I swear—or I'd like to believe—I'd gun them down
to see your life break through that moment and go on carving
the way for us to follow. And yes, my sister, I know
that this is just helpless-man thinking, that the water
rolling along means your life was an imperative
for us to look ahead to the next turn, singing.
But here you are, drinking coffee with your mamá,

here you are, insisting: *we are only human; of course
we have real fears, but that doesn't mean we are going
to be paralyzed by them,* and I want to leap
into the film as into swift water to save you, you
who saved the river.

On Strike

Elizabeth A. Tomanio

The clouds are not behaving how clouds should.
They joined the trees on a silent strike,
ceasing to act as a barrier. Trees
not uprooted for lumber have absorbed
a third less carbon dioxide
in a decade. We continue exhaling.
The waters warm,
fish do not spawn,
and polar bears lose their home.

We do not all begin riding bikes to work.
We order online,
receive meals and gifts
in boxes overflowing
with cellophane.
We go hiking and leave plastic waste behind
after our consumption.
History demonstrates
we care for causes
only when the tiny terrariums
we exist within
do not receive the light or heat needed
to create a water cycle
for our photosynthesis.
We cannot see past the glass walls,
look beyond our own reflections,
to places unfamiliar
and barely surviving.

Sheltering in Place

Tony Fusco

We are the acorn people hiding within hard shells

We are the tree people alive behind walls of bark
We are the oyster men with a pearl within

We are a juicy peach woman, seed inside
the cradle of the pit
We are the potato people buried in dirt

We are a ziplocked nation

We are a preserved people, sealed in mason jars
We are feathered hens inside the coop

We are sleeping bears in caves

We are ants in a social underground
We are an archived generation enclosed
in photo albums layered in plastic stacks

Thoroughbred stallions in stable stalls

Shakespearian sonnets housed between
the plaster bookends

Hermit monks cloistered within our scholarship
and prayers

We are an Inuit people in houses of hard ice

We are souls in a body's solitary confinement

But-Heads

Marilyn Nelson

I know—everyone does—what we should do
to breathe life back into our Mother Earth,
but it's probably too late anyway
to stop this runaway locomotive,
though great whales writhe in sonar agonies
echoed by the small swan-songs of the bees.
I know what human people have to do
to keep the Earth's other peoples' cycles
of birth, food, reproduction, food, and death
from stopping cold, but I live way out here
in the sticks, where you have to have a car.
I know travel is part of the problem,
but I have friends on other continents
and miles to go before I let age win.
I know my diet is factory-farmed:
eggs laid by de-beaked hens, bananas grown
by workers pesticides have made sterile.
But it's pointless to go against the flow,
isn't it? Anyway, what can I do?
I know we're poisoning land and water,
but change my life? I love my new iPhone!

We're but-heads, sliding toward oblivion,
roped together like hapless mountaineers,
like lovers sworn to a suicide pact.

Assassins

Alexandrina Sergio

Some 540 million years back
we wriggled in the sea,
wide-mouthed floating things with
(according to fossil study)
no anus,
making us not unlike
the plastic bags
we now cast back
into our birthplace–
an act very like lacing the
family-picnic lemonade
with rat poison
or hiring an assassin
to take out grandmother.

Trespassers at Morgan Point

Vivian Shipley

Cautious as a stag leading does into a clearing, two fishermen look
    toward the house, just checking. As if crossing a lawn they had
newly seeded, their steps are shortened, rods held low.

Heading for the black rocks, one holds the hand of his son, knowing
    full well their Zodiac is beached above high water on the pink
granite. Not trying to claim they are lost, confused or sorry,

it's anger that simmers in their throats, idling like an outboard motor
    as I point to: *Private Property*. A United jet taking off from
Tweed New Haven censors bitch. No Roger Tory Peterson,

these two won't teach the boy to tell a snowy egret from a white heron
    by an egret's black bill, black legs and yellow feet. Busy popping
caps off Rolling Rock, the father doesn't point to another egret

shuffling feet about in order to stir up shiners, a habit white herons
    don't have. Teaching his son to break bottles for sea glass, he calls
a cormorant *crow* as it spreads wings like an eagle. We're all

trespassers of one sort or another but that does it. I dial East Haven
    police to demand protection. Then I gloat while snapper after
snapper jumps as if drawn by a magnet into the cove. Badge or no

badge, I know these two fishermen will resurface, the boy carrying
    beer. On good days, or bad, they'll be back. If rip tide feathers
the Sound, it will be a sign to them, irrepressible as tide.

Cruising

Steve Straight

for Tony Hoagland

We're standing on the top deck of the *Apocalypse*,
Prestige Level, its wastewater fouling the sea in our wake
as off in the distance the moonlit iceberg of awareness
pokes through the surface of our comprehension,
though ninety percent of it lurks below.

Ten percent is about all we can take
yet still not enough to change our ways,
not enough to link the polar bear stranded on its tiny floe
to the steak, medium-rare, on our bone china plate,

the zooplankton ingesting the molecules of plastic bag
we used yesterday to cart home the romaine lettuce
grown in the sunny concentration camp
of the Salinas Valley,

lobsters scuttling north to cooler water
as longhorned ticks bushwhack their way
into new territory, the heroes of some other story,
while we buy clothing treated with permethrin
or spray our kids with DEET
to think ourselves safe from the viruses.

Down south, the mangroves know all this,
their roots knitted together in a fiber-optic system,
collecting and sharing data from their leaves,
doing their best to excrete excess salt or store it in their tissues,
stabilizing shorelines and taming tsunamis
until it's all too much, even for experts.

Can you hear the musicians?
The ones asked to soothe all the passengers?
Years from now they will find one of the rosewood violins,
surprisingly pristine, and exhibit it in the Museum of Civilization.

Storm Advisory

Susannah Lawrence

Do you hear that wind? Bees, thousands of bees. Do you think the red oak is safe? Some heavy thing moved out there, roused. I'm sure of it. How can you sleep? The dogs barked at the east window, raced to the north one, won't settle. What do they know? The wind's tearing at the trees, shredding them in pieces. When I shake your shoulder, it feels loose. Clouds barrel past, strobe the moon. Dark again. No lights in the valley. Is our power on? I'm going to wake you. Isn't that the siren? Isn't it going too long? I can barely hear over the wind. It sounds like fire-roar. What happened last time? What did they do? Did we ever find those instructions? Oh, there's the rain. It smells strange—oil? plastic? not like wet grass. Aren't you awake yet? So many trees in danger. You're mumbling. I can't read your face. Better to stay, to go? Did you lock the door? I'm trying to remember when we planted the basswood, the two birches, the elm for Owen. They're ok, aren't they? You still love me, don't you? There, there it is again, closer. Did you hear it this time? Will no one tell us when? Why will no one say where it's safe? We did everything we could, didn't we, didn't we?

Getting to Prayer
Patricia Horn O'Brien

I'd given up saying Grace since it'd become clear
God had left the room of this universe. With no one
and nothing to thank but my own industry, my decision
to pull up my chair, I sank back and forked food without thought.

That was my phase of existential angst, and it didn't last.
Now it suits me more to think of the path
my supper took, backward from the field greens on
my stoneware plate, to the refrigerator Shoreline Appliance

sold and delivered, the driver's neck wrapped
in a paisley do-rag, his back drenched, nevertheless. The drink
I offered barely cold enough for a man
hauling refrigerators. Next, to the market at Stop & Shop,

the crooked young man with a crooked spine (and other-
wise perfectly fine) sweeping corn silk and tracked-in sand…
   It is summer and somewhere there's a beach.
    Somewhere an ocean…

from around the feet of the produce man, who dismantles
his tower of lettuce in crackling plastic stacks from
cart-to-cold counter. I heard him talk
with another aproned man stacking pineapples,

each one a tribute to a distant sun, about
the looming threat of a walk-out. They shrug and
never lose the rhythm of their work. You can tell me
I'm reading in too much. But then

there's the truck. An 18-wheeler with a cab big enough
for sleeping and perhaps a girlfriend to overturn the loneliness
of the long haul's drone. But it's there I am stymied. Who,
with a stoneware dish upon a woven table cloth, can

imagine the act of harvesting endless rows of delicate leaves
stretched across fields of rain and the bitter sun
on either side of rain that grows all that's green and batters
those who bend to pick an eternity of lettuce? Amen.

Catawba

Benjamin S. Grossberg

They do it overnight, the catawba tendrils,
reach and wrap the wire above them—
grow and curl, extend and expand. They reach
blindly because how else could they reach?
And find what they didn't know was there,
what's been arranged for them, the perfect
structure for their needs. Or as perfect
as this man could make it. What happens
in darkness, in a single evening—
let's not call it passion, not compare it
to human bodies, which also can reach, unseeing,
for each other; let's not think how conducive
the fixation. If I decide a tendril's not
landed right, I can undo it—carefully—maybe
half the time. The other times result
in damage. Let's not call it passion, not
compare it to how men can hold each other
in the dark, can coil each other's bodies
in a green fastness, the interlocking of a desire
more fierce than simple need. We know need;
we pass its debased currency daily. We know
what blandness its worship comes to. But do we
know this? Overnight, the instinctive triple
coil of a thin tendril, such fierce binding?
Let's not call it passion, not be implicated
in its dumb green living; not take it as just
another reminder from the natural world
of too much mind, how often it fails us.

Not Children

Benjamin S. Grossberg

I know. But let me describe how gently
I pulled apart the plastic, the cowl, how the plastic
split at its stapled seam, revealing wet, olive-
colored bark. I'm not exaggerating when I say
I've never seen anything more beautiful
in the human body, though it did most resemble
human skin. Let me talk about the winnowing
of fingers through barrows of the local clay
cut with composted horse manure, fingers, arms
up to the elbow, sifting, mixing, breaking up
clumps of the compost, feathering it over
heavy clay, aerating, leavening, darkening.
Let me describe the speckled brown:
how the mixed medium had richness, felt good
on the palms, soft on the soft parts of the body.
Now imagine yourself bending with me,
lifting a tree from the plastic, extricating a single
sapling from the bundle, how your fingers
relearn gentleness unlacing the hair of the roots
from other roots, how in the manner of a mother
washing a child, you touch the most vulnerable
parts of the tree, the places where it would be
frighteningly easy to choke off life. And now
let's stand together, lift it from the plastic
and wash it down again, the pressure of the hose
blocked by your palm, so water falls easily
on the young trunk. Its place in the world is prepared;
bring it over, rest it in, as if into human arms.
The earth will love the thing no more than we do.
And now imagine yourself with me
stepping back from the planted sapling. Feel
how you steep and rise, how your chest fills
and then the slow, steady release of air.

Forage

Luisa Caycedo-Kimura

I turn clay soil, mound rocks,
squeeze grubs with my fingers.
My spade, the soil, a rasp.
A dry northeast heat wave.

When I was five, Mamá chopped
my hair. *Niña salvaje, wild child,*
always in a tangle. Holes in your jeans,
grass stains on your sweaters.

Through my hair, wind, dust, twigs.

Impatient bumblebees,
you know we'll have flowers.

I pull quack grass,
plant deep-rooted cowpeas, mustard,
crimson clover.

Watch for the stealth
of a screech owl in flight.

Write a letter
to my dead mamá.

How does one awaken
this conflicted land?

Last night—a black bear
in the neighbor's pool.
Last night, I almost held berries
for it in my hands.

Hand Tilling

Aaron Caycedo-Kimura

He chuffs his shovel   into soil   with the sole
of his right boot   more dried mud than leather

he balances full weight   both feet   on the shoulders
of the shovel   gloved hands rocking the handle   blade

prying packed clay   he levers a clod   turns it
hacks it   repeats down an eight-foot row   to his right

the smell of earth takes him back   to San Gabriel   the family
farm of rented acreage   before the War   before
Executive Order 9066   eviction   incarceration

after tilling four beds   he plants the shovel   upright
like a gnomon   marking time   rests on the pine bench

under the pin oak   he takes a swig from a can of Coors
surveys his garden   never needs to look   beyond his fence

Arboriculture

Amy Nawrocki

I'm sure the red mulch
spread beneath the dormant azalea
has in its loamy peat the macerated remnants
of a massive Louisiana cypress.
I know it in my bones.

Somewhere in the swamps
of Atchafalaya, an ancient
colossus towering hundreds of feet
was felled with the unheard echo
of a stolen temple bell. The harvested

trophy died again at the mill,
chomped to confetti by the grimacing
false teeth of a machine. I suffer
the russet sin with my arms elbow-deep
in agriculture as I distribute

the ground cover around sweet William
and verbena blossoms in the front yard.
I'm hardly as wicked with those;
their plastic trays were purchased
from the farm stand where tiny, ripe

organic strawberries pleased my lips
and sour cherries melted like wine
lozenges in my mouth. I spit the pits
out the car window on the drive home.
But I am wicked to the core,

and today the supermarket is closer
to the mail drop and the library
where mediocre books, half-read
are overdue, and those bags of the dirty fill
stacked on the concrete walkway near the store

seem so utilitarian, so earthy
and convenient, plus I hate the weeds

which the bag promises to squelch,
and the neighbor, with her elegant
foxgloves and blooming geraniums
is really to blame for this. But I cannot

loose the swamp cypresses
from my mind, these conifers, these
sacred fellows holding the soil in
with their gracious roots, exhaling
with delicate silence. I feel like God

doling out the flood waters,
my bloody hands handsomely disguised
by garden gloves. I am a fraud, a pirate,
and when the levees break again
I will sink into counterfeit soil and drown.

It is a full green morning before the death of George Floyd

Davyne Verstandig

I am working from my perch just below the treetops
seeing into leaves—below
lilies of the valley hide beneath
spreading bleeding hearts,
waiting to be picked and placed on my window altar
where violets and forget-me nots once held a place

a single purple iris sits beside Kuan Yin
she who hears the cries of the world—
the scent of the lilacs by the blue door fainter
spring green darkens
a late spring—June arriving in a few days

And I am something like happy here in this green quiet.

In the Middle Lane, Leaving New Haven

Dolores Hayden

Dusk hovers behind the billboard,
"We Want Your Scrap Gold,"
behind the imported oil on the tank farm,
the rusting metal on the export pier,
the oversize flags on the auto dealer's lot.

Four out of five commuters drive alone.
In the left lane, a black bus
shrink-wrapped with characters for luck
hurtles past me toward the casino.
On the right, a white limo
accelerates to a wedding.
Side by side, we surge past
the hill leveled for a mall.

Who is the risk-taker looking for grace?

A cell tower marks frolic talk
as I exit toward narrow roads
that wind and rise and fall.
I steer into the shapes of time:
River Street, Water Street
curve with fishermen's work,
Leete's Island Road weaves
where farmers grew salt hay
and the last of the light
fades on bone-colored spartina.

Who is the survivor mapping history?

On Colonial Road, a developer
has been clearing for new houses.
Dispossessed, a doe and a buck
wander onto the asphalt—
pay attention!

Braking hard, headlights high,
I hear an owl.
I might as well be an owl,
hooting at the ice,
lecturing the winter.

Snow coats the sand on the beach,
snow drifts over the sea wall next to the Sound.
On Cove Lane, my house resists
the January wind, windows dark.

My house is as cold as only a widow's can be.
On the porch: shovel, rock salt, firewood.

Urban Aesthetic

Rhonda M. Ward

I ain't got no garden. All I got
Is this stretch of dirt in my shortcut,
A few weeds peekin' up in cross-eyed patches
Lookin' like they wanna be cabbage
Or greens

Ain't no mountains in the ghetto
I do have a purple dress though
that I look majestic in
If I do say so myself

Rollin'plains and fields? Forget it.
Only things rollin' 'round here is them pieces of candy wrappin'
And cigarette butts movin' along on a whim of the wind
On their way to the gutter

But beauty ain't lost on ghetto folk
We got us a foreign language we speak in English
We got hair—natural, fried, and curly
We got soul food and double-dutch
And purple…we got purple

Without Sunglasses Anymore

Frederick-Douglass Knowles II

We used to be best friends. You couldn't wait for me to bolt
off the bus. Toss my books in venture. We were Night and
Noon. Moon and Sun. Nothing I would do without you. Hide
behind that 18th hole. Snatch golf balls. Slip into brooks. Leap
bold streams. BMX my bike over makeshift pyramids. Pick berries.
Play Hide & Go Seek. Hot Peas & Butter. Red Light/Green Light.
Kick The Can. Freeze Tag. Football. And *That's My Car!*

We used to be the best of friends. Rendezvous up Oakwood Knoll.
Run, Catch & Kiss behind Uncas School. Moonbeams bouncing
off bodies. Then I changed. No longer had time. Became too busy.
Complained about the weather. What happened to how we played?
Melrose Park, I'm sorry. I'm sorry I no longer talk to you except
to wipe the tears fallen from God's cries. I'm sorry I don't stare
without sunglasses anymore. I'm sorry a snowstorm sends me inside.

Instead of the front yard. To cookie-cut angels into your frosting.
I'm sorry your daughter Autumn makes leaves fall to feed worms.
And I rake them for aesthetics. We were best friends since kindergarten.
Then I grew. I thought. What I really did was whither. Shrank into
schemes of rich and popular. Ignored your Poplars logged illegally
for corporatocracy. Pollutants dumped into ponds I pitched rocks
into. I used to feed the Ducks with my daughters with you. Now I

duck from Seagulls fertilizing your maternal shore. *Melrose, I'm sorry.*
I miss our Summer bike rides blackening my melanin. I miss your woods.
Jane Arms unfurling into an Equinox. I miss Poison Ivy. Skunk Cabbage.
Pussy Willows. Dandelions. Tadpoles. Black Ants. Red Ants. Black-Red
Ants. Horseflies. Dragonflies. Houseflies. Not Houseflies. But I miss lifting
trashcans watching Maggots *I wanna fly dance.* I miss digging Earthworms
to watch them squirm. Then burrow back into your bosom. I miss seeded

Grapes. Sour Apples. Ripe Tomatoes. Collard Greens. Okra. I miss
Gammy's Rosebush. Now Honeybees vanish with no trace. So who's
going to pollinate your Purple Hibiscus? We used to be best friends
since kindergarten. But when I traded my playground for PlayStation.
Tire tube for YouTube. I never knew I'd miss skyscrapers of uncut
grass. Tickling my inner child. While sleeping under a quilt of dreams.

Squinting without shades. As tiny purple dragons soar your lemon Summer smile. Searching for the friend who built castles from sand.

The Talk

Michael "Chief" Peterson

son it's time we talked about the birds and the bees
first I need you to believe that you too can fly
you must protect your wings from some bees cuz they sting
there's many dangerous animals outside of our nest
they invade our tree because their branch is bigger than ours
so what do you do when animals attack
no sudden movements
they may not understand you when you speak
but they know what fear looks like in that invites them closer
so close your mouth and open your eyes
see if you can tell what hives these bees come from
not all of them sting
but I'm guessing they've seen your wings
so they know you can fly and sing
and they can only fly and buzz
so they try and bust your shell before you've fully hatched
this concrete jungle is full of traps
There's many snakes in the streets
that hide in plain sight
and invite you to trust and believe in them
but they're bluffing their chameleons
they never show their true colors but attack you because of yours
so I must teach you to defend yourself
your tone of voice can resolve problems caused by your tone of skin
it's your words that will spare you
some animals lack the integrity to interact with the intelligent
so they use intimidation to scare you
but you will stand firm
you will be smart enough to know
that sometimes the early bird loses his worm to the bully
but you will take no bull
and learn to claw your way out the pits
it's a dog eat dog world
where uniformed K9s are ready to sink their teeth into your dreams
but they only attack if you threaten their pride
I mean hives
no you don't have 9 lives
you're just viewed as that black cat with bad luck

what sucks is if you ever get bit they can just weasel their way out of it
but back to these bees
They earn their stripes by putting you in them
some see black and white instead of wrong and right
if you type why do bees attack into the worldwide spider web
it says and I quote "experience has shown Bees tend to attack dark things"
now that stings
but I guess it just is what it is
where we're from we learn to dance with wolves and we hide from pigs
so what do you do when animals attack
you stand your ground
spread your wings slowly
speak softly
tell them you are still learning to fly
that you only fight with your words not your fists
but you've seen this happen to too many of your flock
and that with you it may not stop
but one day it will end
if you should die today then God will mend your wings in heaven
I told you in the beginning you must believe that you too can fly
so remind these buzzards
that once they sting you
the bee instantly begins to die too

Wasted Lives

Pegi Deitz Shea

Addis Ababa, March 11, 2017

Outside Ethiopia's capital, the Repi land fill—
full of 50 years of refuse,
home to thousands of poor displaced
by high rises—mounts and mounts
until it cannot anymore, and the waste
avalanches, eliminating scores of lives.

Ambassadors of the African Union live
in the pricey city, taking their fill
of fashion, food and fun. They waste
time debating, while they refuse
to deal with the people who mount
the garbage, foraging for treasures, say, misplaced

remotes or uneaten crusts. They call the place
Koshe, meaning "dust," meaning lives
disintegrate beneath these mounts,
meaning sloughed skin cells fill
surrounding huts, meaning material refuse
abides with its own kind: human waste.

Some blame the collapse on plastic waste;
others blame the people who placed
their homes too close, who refuse
to live "acceptable" lives.
The poor blame those whose pockets are filled;
they claim ecological discrimination; they mount

protests against economic injustice; they mount
tiny caskets on their shoulders. This waste
of life *this* way is not new. In 2000, the Payatas landfill
landslide, the Java avalanche in 2005. Guatemala City places
the whole country's trash higher in priority than the 7000 lives
who breathe noxious gases released by its refuse,

who fight the fires caused by methane, who refuse
to conveniently die for what amounts
to a pittance in taxes. Let's examine our lives:
In the North End of Hartford, our mountain of waste
is housed under a guise of grass; New York City placed
its trash in Fresh Kills, Staten Island; China fills

and sends barges with bulging amounts of waste
to sea, where microfibers and plastic refuse replace
lives in the marine food chain...our seafood...our fill.

A Cliché in the Projects

José B. González

So much of a cliché, that sunflower in front of H6,
our apartment in the projects where the soil

was so rough that barefoot kids would rub their
feet after hopscotching in front of our door.

That cliché took wandering Wiffle balls to the neck
and still stood stiff, barely a scratch. Back then,

cops would walk or run by, chasing a name,
and that cliché just minded its own, even when

they caught the boy who shot Charlie. The third
summer that the cliché came back, I started

to notice a couple of other apartments had
a flower or two in front of their doors. Mrs.

Johnson even had a one-foot flimsy fence
around her geraniums. After we moved

out, I would go out of my way to check out
the apartment. Each time, the sunflower

had grown so much that I swore I was
shrinking. I don't go around there anymore

but the other day I read a story in our local
newspaper about an arrest next door

to our old H6. The article didn't say anything
about sunflowers. But maybe the writer just

doesn't believe in clichés the way I do,
the way some families have to.

And Then I Read About

José B. González

Another confession. Before she left
      Earth, I never asked her to teach
me about Earth, so I read books
      about planting, and I learned
about water, and how much was
      too little and how much could kill
the roots, and I understood why
      she left El Salvador's earthquakes,
and then I started to read books
      about soil, and how crops should
be moved, and I understood why she
      had no choice but to move Yani and
me, and then I read about landslides,
      and I understood why she brought
her mother and her sister to live
      with us, and then I read about
deforestation and how only Haiti
      was worse than our old country,
and then I remembered how they said
      that she looked toward the sky
when she took her last breath,
      and then I looked at the trees
and saw what her eyes had dreamed.

The Call of the Void

Jonathan Andersen

I was seven, leaning into the wind on
      the bluff twenty feet or so above surging,

retreating waves—something snagged in
      my breath, radiating like voltage

through my chest, into my skinny
      arms, legs—I craned my neck

shaking, this terrifying new possibility: two
      me's and one wanted to step out

into the high salt air. As Americans we have
      no word or phrase for this yearning wired

to the leap and fall, but last night as we lay
      awake listening to the walls tick

with insects, you told me the French call it
      l'appel du vide. Now here you

and I stand at the edge of the garden we planted in
      blistering spring heat—into this life I still

love—and watch new beetles flock to, then mass
      upon squash blossoms. The

goldfinch—here like a spark, a coulomb of
      sun in this squally afternoon—darts and

darts back, hops and flits, tells us what we
      already know: there is no

backing or turning away, no
      shrugging off: only holding hands we

follow the whole human race, step
    into the swollen sun and storms of

whatever this will be

Zone 6

John Surowiecki

Our silver irises ring in the void.
The rest of the garden's fine, the pines,
fine, although we're still afraid an ICBM
might drop out of the sky and land
in the middle of our Siberians.
Meanwhile, a chainsaw
chokes somewhere, and sleek
dogs eat meat in a gulp.
Wary of the beasts
we take shovels with us
when we get the mail
and when we're tired from
digging we lean on them,
wondering if our sanguineas
will hemorrhage one day
in a new hot zone
or if our blue flags will ever
find hospices of shade
before everything changes
and gardens retreat from
our ability to see them.
No one will ever know we
planted those irises. The first
peony was ours too, and the cherry tree
and the tulip tree with inexact leaves
like those drawn by children.
We laid a carpet of myrtle,
imagined the reach of lilacs,
theorized what nature would be like
if it lived in the vacuum it abhors.
Now we dig beds for the children
of the children of strangers
or for a drought that rises to its source
and sinks to the molten core of the earth,
making dust of irises and irises,
bearded and beardless, of dust.

When I Call It the Zombie Apocalypse, Neither of Us Is as Scared as We Should Be

Jennifer A. Payne

for my nephew Max

At dawn, I scoop soft flesh from native squash
separate the slippery seeds in a shallow dish,
add olive oil, salt, pepper   wonder
should I dry them, save them, hide them
instead in a dark corner in the cellar store?

Before too much time, I should teach you,
teach you these things you'll need to know
like where the wild asparagus grow
and how to shuck oysters   if they remain

Scientists say now the seals might die.
Will oysters follow suit? The sweet brine of clams the same?
Do I even know if seeds will store and for how long
before they   and we   amount to ash?

Once, an acorn took root in the cellar,
stretched its albino shoot as high as it could reach
then gave up the ghost with a long heavy sigh
that haunted the house for days.

Acorns, I am told, are edible   with work
But I pray that won't be you, your sweet small self
stretched reaching-thin towards the sun
     or the rain   or the last nut high on a branch.

Remind me to tell you about nuts,
and roots and berries, spring shoots,
and mushrooms—both kinds, just in case.

After Us

Louis Gabordi

When the fever breaks, time will pass as it always has,
in rising and ebbing tides of light, tireless and without pause,
indifferent to what remains and what has gone.
However sudden or slow our leaving, no one can say
this patient earth will not again be paradise.

She may in only decades heal her lesser wounds.
The abraded plains will green again in summers,
their tall grasses teeming with the urgent labors and
intrigues of whatever creatures may survive us.
The blistered beds of siphoned marshes will melt
and breathe again beneath dark tea water.

Gravity, relentless as time, will buckle the rusting
bones of buildings rising through the clouds and
snap the careful arcs of bridges until stone and steel
release and rain on everything below. Metallic moons,
blind and silent in decaying orbits, will fall into the sea.
Even our pervasive plastic shards will slowly dissipate
in sunlight or lie buried under yards of marine snow.

And when our peculiar noises, latent in the hovering brass
of tower bells and fuel tanks waiting for a jagged spark
are heard a final time, and when the elemental dust
that was our bodies is taken by the wind and water,
neither sound nor scent will remain of us to trigger flight,
and the last trace of encoded wariness of a lost species
will disappear from the blood of the newborn fawn.

It will be as if we never were at all.

Climate Change Quartet

David K. Leff

> *Trees and stones will teach you that which you can never learn from masters. —Saint Bernard*

1. Glacial Boulder

Forged in fire when Earth was young,
wrenched loose from my home ledge far north,
I was ground down in a river of ice, locked
for centuries in a womb frigid and dark.

Melting slowly, the glacier lost its grip,
orphaned me on a barren slope pierced by light,
strewn with jumbled scree, leaving
me whipped and shaped by restless wind.

I waited and waited, and waited more,
for I am made of time as much
as solidified molten minerals
once smoldering with the heat of eons.

Resting quietly in the woods,
I know millennia like you feel minutes
for clocks and calendars fail in unbearable
expanses of countless seasons.

Untold ages tattooed me with lichens,
gathered a company of grasses, ferns and conifers
before the coming of birch, maple, and beech
whose snaking roots split me in two.

First peoples took me for a pulpit,
my angled overhang offering shelter.
Farmers carved chunks for foundations, and charcoal
colliers slept beside me with smudgy fires.

Smoke and exhausts now corrupt time itself,
ripening epochs to centuries and centuries
to decades passing like years
until moments dissolve and lose their meaning.

2. Lichen

We were brazen pioneers, finding the boulder's
roughened granitic hide a perfect purchase
in long ago barren days, before trees, birds
or squirrels. Naked and lonely, we dressed
it in jaunty style—lacy leafy
crenellations in sporty grays and greens.

Seemingly plant-like, our shrewd conspiracy
of fungi and algae is the ineffable soul of problem-
solving collaboration. Fed by rain, dust,
and sunlight we flourish in clean air,
fade in smoke, erratic rainfall, and warming.

Fragile underfoot, we are tougher than stone,
subversive chemical secretions slowly, ever
so slowly dissolving the boulder's
impenetrable stuff to mineral soil sustaining life.
But as warmth creeps north like an invisible heat-
glacier, we'll waste away before our work is done.

3. Yellow Birch

In deep woods on bony ground
where roots contort to seek small pockets
of soil and moisture, our congregation of birch,
maple, hemlock and beech grow thick
around the grand boulder on hubbly ground
sloping in several directions.

I've a tropism leaning toward the western
sun, a twisted root wedged into a frost
crack in the great rock's backside, my trunk
shiny yellow-silver and lichen splotched, horizontal
bands peeling in thin flossy curls, buds popping,
leaves falling with the regular order of seasons.

Cut for farmhouse cookfires, barn
timbers and fenceposts, clearcut for charcoal
and tanbark, we trees return in generational
tenacity, sprouting from stumps and seeds

with homes for roosting birds, forage for deer,
sheltering chipmunks, feeding leaf chewing insects.

Rot is beautiful! Autumn leaves, fallen
branches and toppled trunks sustain
us with humus in turn nourishing humanity.
I'll persist until my time's done, but winged seeds
riding warming winds will find cooler
spots far north where our boulder was born.

4. Hermit Thrush

Timing is everything and ever more
chancy under shifting skies exhaling southerly breath.

Brown-backed, chest spotted,
I've a sporty tail-flick, sing with liquid
fluting, or scold with a sharp *tuk-tuk-tuk*
among birch and hemlock, nesting in the boulder's
shadow, a cup of leaves, grass and lichen.

But early springs now beckon with capricious
temper to nest at higher latitudes and altitudes
where earthworms, beetles, and ants
might be ill-timed for meals, and nestlings
could freeze in spasmodic cold snaps.

Planetary clocks are out of kilter,
the synchronicity of seasons just fly-by-night.

5. Boulder Reprise

Call me dumb as a rock, cold and silent
as stone, but I'm rock solid, steady,
emboldened, a stone whose stories you'll leave
unturned only to risk rock bottom.

Little River Elegy

Brad Davis

1.

Rublev's angels have no perfection in
and of themselves but only what is lent
them—as it is with all created things:
the oak in the icon, the Little River

below our condo in wooded Putnam,
the cat asleep through the morning's riot
of hummingbirds. Hummingbirds! Like Milton's
rebels angling for the right to rule.

But we are not among the likes of Andrei's
three angels who face and sweetly honor
one another. Our neighbors are Picasso's
troupe of six, stalled in a void where no one

faces anyone. And this is our call:
to be among them as a little river
or sweetwater-filled feeder or as rain—
to be for nurture. Or naught. Have mercy.

2.

Just north of us, a line of stately trees:
broadleaf, coniferous, and here and there
an invasive vine insinuating
with a will to overwhelm the planet.

Do I exaggerate? You judge. I know
only the ease with which I can kill
a wasp or roach or spider trespassing
in my personal space. I am not proud

of this, but well cognizant of devils
among the angels and the need to sweep
a room with martial regularity.
The overreaching vines must be removed.

The line between anger and responsive
stewardship is leaf and litter covered.
I must take care how I investigate
lest, unknowing, I do harm. Have mercy.

3.

I'm of two minds: one child-like, naive,
capable of huge leaps of believing,
persuaded prayer makes miracles happen;
the other, well assured nothing matters,

we being self-deceived, disease-inclined,
death-destined organisms, full stop.
No surprise I love what quiets my thoughts
or overwhelms them: an ocean of ferns

on my thighs like angels' fingers; that view
from the ferry—Rockland to Vinalhaven—
its gallery of glacial art and sea;
even the rush of the elicit—how

for hours, here and there, I can forget
the dissonance tearing at my brain. Best,
it seems, to be a little river free
and clear of all contending narratives.

4.

Life above the Little River is good.
The little river, in and of itself,
is good. As it was created to be.
And there is that of us which is also

good, though we have made a mess of things
and need help to make it right: each other
and, say, wisdom from above. For we are
not as hummingbirds programmed to fight

for food and nesting sites, rather we are
free to work it out peaceably, to dance
and tell self-effacing jokes and linger
quietly around an evening table

and love our so-called enemies. Who would
ever guess this of us, looking at our
histories of war? But why ever look there?
Life above the Little River is good.

5.

In this world, indeed: quartered above
the Little River in busy Putnam,
bivouacked among saints and scoundrels and all
who sleep the sleep of death, going back

to who first encamped along these streams.
Haunt of hummingbirds, the occasional
bobcat, mink, eagle, bear—the place is rich
with life and us, who tip it all toward naught.

O wisdom, here indeed we carry on
for now. From where you sit, I hope to God
our sentience is not irrelevant
or something shortlisted for erasure.

Are you the one to whom prayer should ascend?
I wish only for the good of what is
just and pure—lovely—making no demands.
Only say the word. Only guide our hands.

Irrevocable

Margaret Gibson

::
  Someone no longer alive

is hovering over a great expanse of smartweed, panic grass, and midden
where a house used to be

              where trees and gardens once flourished

where puddles and ponds held a sky of clouds and stars
in place

        for a moment

and you lived there…Ah, my dear

::
I speak from the liminal space where your beloved's last barely audible

        breath slipped into your body

then out the window into the winter chill, whose horizon line rolled up

        as if it were twine

into a point, a still point—

                a full stop that opens the heart

From that point, I speak

::
As once you washed the body of your beloved
let us wash

        for the last time

this one earth, this only, and only once, for once and for all earth

        as if it were a lover who has died

and we, not knowing what to do

at last must wash the poles, north and south where long ago the ice
cracked open
                    sheared off
                              and melted

Last, the mountain peaks

Last, the crowns of oaks and maples, on whose bare branches long
          strips of torn plastic flutter

Also the steeples, the turrets, the domes

Last, the open fields and meadows, wash them clean

the vast desert and its last oasis

riverbeds and shrunken rills

ravines and gullies

the rocky promontories from which we viewed the sea
as it rose to cover the cities
                              Last, the cities

submerged full fathom or in low tide only the towers and the tips
          of the high-rises winking up

Last, the sidewalks, shop windows, market stalls

Last, pebble, shell, and skull

Last, lark

and satellite, wash them, and the field of broken mirrors

Last, the house

Last, the bed

Last, the hills of midden, and their treasures

a button

a seed

a feather

a zipper

a chip of china plate

Last, the nose cone, the black box

Last, the trawler, the landing gear, the microchip, the missing part

Last the kiva, the sweat lodge, the drum

Last, the prayer rugs, the pews, the cushions

Last, the seat of enlightenment beneath what remains of a small tree's
      spreading canopy

Last, the factories, the foundries, the mills

the maze of subway tunnels

the turnstiles

Last, the eye of the needle through which we could not pass

Last, a gun, a mine, a missile

Last, a bridge

Last, middle C on the piano, last a cello, a violoncello, in particular the
      Sonata for Violoncello no.2 in D, op. 64, by Heinrich
      von Herzogenberg

precious because it was the last music you listened to

precious because, like the last word your beloved spoke, you did not
      know it was last

Last, the pattern of fish displayed on ice, and their many-eyed, one-
        eyed gaze

Last, the last whale beached on the shore at Truro

Last, the glint of an eye in the periwinkle, the lovely, sinuous ripple
        of a reclusive snake

Last, the chemicals, the vitamins, the pills, the chemicals

Last, a hearing aid

a pair of binoculars

a surgeon's knife, a sling, a robotic hand

Last, to list only a few from the multitude that perished, fox and
        laughing gull, swallowtail and hawk

  lion panther giraffe mosquito trillium hummingbird hibiscus owl

Last, the very last line in a poem by Rilke
the line
        you can't forget the ache of, the line you didn't enact

not one syllable of it—
          You must change your life

::
Space, of course, lasts

I walk upon it, as one would walk on a tablecloth for a table
        no one will set

What's left of my eyesight has dimmed, what I hear is only wind
        and that, muted

And because I have nothing to write on, I build cairn after cairn

lifting stones, balancing them

touching what remains in place, as if it were a new alphabet,
    or a sentence in Braille

You are reading the last of the earth's last rivers and mountains
    do you know that?

These stones, these silences

the last words

held in mind for a moment—

as if they were a net of fireflies shimmering in a summer field
    one can't tell apart from a night sky and stars

Wash them
                each stone, each firefly

wash them clean

this one, a love cry

that one, lament

and the last one the wing of a warning you might still be able to hear

just as once, long ago
you caught the smoke of the oracle rising from a rift zone

at the center of the earth

::
If these cairns, these stone syllables, survive, there may be no one left
to read the poem they make—

but if by chance, there is…

let the stones be read aloud, so that a human voice

might widen its reach, floating off to the stars like the ringing-through
    of a great bronze bell

like the audible layers of birdsong gradually moving west as dawn brightens, or used to

and the great earth turns

About the Poets

Denise Abercrombie's work has appeared in *Minnesota Review, Fireweed, Connecticut Review, Phoebe: Journal of Feminist Scholarship, Theory and Aesthetics, The Lumberyard: A Radio Magazine, Struggle, Writing on the Edge, Yale Global Health Review,* and elsewhere. The director of Fine Arts at E.O. Smith High School in Storrs, Denise teaches theater and helps coordinate Curbstone Foundation's Poetry in the Julia de Burgos Park series in Willimantic, Connecticut.

Jonathan Andersen is a professor of English at Quinebaug Valley Community College. His most recent book of poems, *Augur,* (Red Dragonfly Press 2018), received the David Martinson–Meadowhawk Prize and was named a finalist for the Connecticut Book Award in Poetry.

Christine Beck is a poet, educator, and a former board member of The Connecticut Poetry Society, where she founded its educational series, Poets on Poetry. Her publications include *Blinding Light* (Grayson Books 2013), *I'm Dating Myself* (Dancing Girl Press 2015), and *Stirred, Not Shaken,* (Five Oaks Press 2016). She is a former Poet Laureate of West Hartford, Connecticut. Her website is http://ChristineBeck.net.

Terry Bohnhorst Blackhawk: Currently living in Connecticut, Terry Bohnhorst Blackhawk is Founding Director (1995-2015) of Detroit's InsideOut Literary Arts Project. Awards include the 2010 Pablo Neruda Prize and the 2003 John Ciardi Prize for *Escape Artist,* her second volume of poems. A frequent Michigan Audubon volunteer, Blackhawk's fifth collection *One Less River* (2019) was named a top environmental title by *The Revelator* and a *Kirkus Reviews* Best Poetry Title.

Aaron Caycedo-Kimura was born in Santa Rosa, California. His poetry appears or is forthcoming in *Beloit Poetry Journal, Poet Lore, DMQ Review, Tule Review, Louisiana Literature,* and elsewhere. He is the winner of the 2020 Slapering Hol Press Chapbook Competition and is a recipient of a Robert Pinsky Global Fellowship in Poetry.

Luisa Caycedo-Kimura is a Colombian-born writer, translator, and educator. Her honors include a John K. Walsh Residency Fellowship at the Anderson Center, an Adrienne Reiner Hochstadt Fellowship at Ragdale, and a Robert Pinsky Global Fellowship in Poetry. Her work has also been nominated for the Pushcart Prize. A former attorney, Luisa left the legal profession to pursue her passion for writing. She holds an MFA from Boston University.

Luisa's poems appear or are forthcoming in *The Cincinnati Review, Sunken Garden Poetry 1992-2011, RHINO, Shenandoah, Mid-American Review*, and elsewhere.

Carol Chaput's collection of poems, *Field Notes*, was published by Dogwood Press. Her work appears in poetry publications including *Potpourri, Calliope, The Red Fox Review, Earth Day Poems (CT-DEP)*, and *Stray Branch*. She was the recipient of the Mark Van Doren Poetry Award.

Ginny Lowe Connors is the author of several poetry collections, including *Toward the Hanging Tree: Poems of Salem Village*. Her chapbook, *Under the Porch*, won the Sunken Garden Poetry Prize. Connors has also edited a number of poetry anthologies. She is the co-editor of *Connecticut River Review*. Her poem "Stone Harvest" was inspired by the beautiful old stone walls she encounters on walks in rural northeastern Connecticut.

Robert Cording has published nine books of poems, the latest of which is *Without My Asking*. Poems have recently appeared in *Best American Poetry, Hudson Review, Georgia Review, Southern Review, New Ohio Review*, and *The Common*. Cording has received two NEA fellowships in poetry.

Brad Davis moved to Putnam, Connecticut, in June 2019. That summer he acquainted himself with the Little River and its history, from its source in Woodstock to where it joins the Quinebaug in Putnam. Recent poem placements include *Brilliant Corners, LETTERS, Fielder's Choice, Willimantic Chronicle*, and *Journal of the American Medical Association*.

Cortney Davis is the author of four poetry collections, most recently *I Hear Their Voices Singing: Poems New & Selected*. Her honors include an NEA Poetry Fellowship, three Connecticut Commission on the Arts Poetry Grants, the Prairie Schooner Poetry Prize, and a Tillie Olsen Creative Writing Award. Davis is poet laureate of Bethel, Connecticut. www.cortneydavis.com

Catherine DeNunzio has published in *Many Mountains Moving; The Breath of Parted Lips: Voices from The Robert Frost Place, Vol. II; Teacher-Writer 2015 (Volume VII); Italian Americana (Summer 2020)*; and *Connecticut Literary Anthology 2020*. A retired teacher and member of the Westerly, Rhode Island, Savoy Poetry Salon, DeNunzio lives in Connecticut with her spouse and their dog.

Joanie DiMartino comments: An ekphrastic piece in response to a painting of the same title by Dominic Vescera Ragosta, "Jump, Jive, and Whale" was also inspired by whale songs I listened to as I wrote. Only male humpback whales express themselves musically, which allowed for a poetic revision of the relationship between whalers and a species they did not hunt. This piece has been performed with whale song.

Daniel Donaghy is the author of three books of poems: *Somerset* (NYQ Books, 2018), which won the 2019 Paterson Poetry Prize; *Start with the Trouble* (University of Arkansas Press, 2009); and *Streetfighting* (BkMk Press, 2005). He is a Professor of English at Eastern Connecticut State University.

James Finnegan has published poems in *Ploughshares, Poetry East, The Southern Review, The Virginia Quarterly Review*, as well as in the anthologies: *Good Poems: American Places* edited by Garrison Keillor; *Open Field*; *Laureates of Connecticut*; *Shadows of Unfinished Things*; and most recently *Imagining Vesalius*. He posts aphoristic ars poetica on the blog *ursprache*: https://ursprache.blogspot.com/

Stanford M. Forrester is a former president of the Haiku Society of America and editor of bottle rockets press, which is celebrating its 22nd year. Forrester's Japanese pen name is "Sekiro." and "Shi Lu" is the Chinese version of "Sekiro."

Jon R. Friedman is the artist whose work is on the cover of this book. His portraits, landscape paintings, and sculptures have been shown in exhibitions throughout the United States. His portrait work is represented in numerous collections here and abroad including seventeen portraits in the permanent collection of the National Portrait Gallery in Washington, DC. More of his work can be seen at www.jonrfriedman.com.

Tony Fusco is Past President of the Connecticut Poetry Society. He has a Master's Degree in Creative Writing from Southern Connecticut State University. Fusco has served as editor of *Caduceus, The Connecticut River Review*, and *Long River Run*, and moderator of the public television program West Shore Poets. He has written five books of poetry: *Jessie's Garden, Droplines, Java Scripture, Extinction*, and *Don't Make Me Laugh*.

Louis Gabordi is a retired educator and mentor to young poets. A member of the Westerly, Rhode Island, Savoy Poetry Salon, he has shared his work in Southeastern Connecticut and Southern Rhode Island. He lives in Ledyard, Connecticut, with his spouse. Nothing so informs his work as his love and concern for the natural world.

Margaret Gibson, the editor of this volume, is the author of 12 books of poems, all from LSU Press, most recently *Not Hearing the Wood Thrush*, 2018. A new book, *The Glass Globe*, is forthcoming in Fall, 2021. Awards include the Lamont Selection for *Long Walks in the Afternoon*, her second book, 1982; the Melville Kane Award (co-winner) for *Memories of the Future*, (1986), and the Connecticut Book Award for *One Body*, 2008. *The Vigil* was a Finalist for the National Book Award in Poetry in 1993. *Broken Cup* was a Finalist for 2016 Poets' Prize, and the title poem from the book won a Pushcart Prize for that year. "Passage," from *Not Hearing the Wood Thrush*, was included in *The Best American Poetry, 2017*. As Connecticut State Poet Laureate (2019-2022) Margaret Gibson has taken as her social focus "Poetry and the Environment during Climate Crisis." She has been awarded an Academy of American Poets Grant for Poet Laureates, 2020-2021. With a portion of this grant, she is funding this very anthology, *Waking Up to the Earth*. She is also funding videos of Connecticut poets reading their poems about the environment in natural settings and also poetry programs in "Green Poetry Cafes." For more information, visit her website: www.margaretgibsonpoetry.com.

D. Walsh Gilbert lives in Farmington, Connecticut and spends mid-summer evenings counting bats which visit at dusk. She's thankful the numbers are increasing. In 2017, she published a chapbook, *Ransom*, which addresses suicide and addiction issues. She's currently secretary of the Riverwood Poetry Series and co-editor of the *Connecticut River Review*, published by the Connecticut Poetry Society.

José B. González is the author of *Toys Made of Rock* and *When Love Was Reels*. His poetry has been published in the *Norton Introduction to Literature* and in journals including *Callaloo*, *Palabra*, and *Acentos Review*. A Fulbright Scholar, he is the co-editor of *Latino Boom: An Anthology of U.S. Latino Literature* and the editor of LatinoStories.com.

Benjamin S. Grossberg is Director of Creative Writing at the University of Hartford. He comments: Written twelve years apart, these poems feel almost like companion pieces. Are plants capable of intimacy? Sciences tells us they communicate and nurture each other to their mutual benefit. Can they share that intimacy with us? While plants can't quite replace husbands or wives (or children), in my experience, love of the vegetal world can be similarly fortifying and familial.

Mary Guitar's poetry is rooted in the natural world, and in art, science, and the intersection of nature and the human spirit. She has published work in several anthologies and journals and is a winner of the Al Savard Memorial

Poetry Competition sponsored by the Connecticut Poetry Society. Guitar is a member of Connecticut River Poets.

Gwen Gunn has had poems published in national and international journals, and she co-edited the poetry journal *Embers*. She has participated in poetry readings in Connecticut and New York City, and with her partner Norman Marshall performs "Poetry's Greatest Hits." She recently won two firsts in the National Confederation of State Poetry Societies contests, one of which was the national Winners Circle Award. Her latest book of poetry is *Tastes*.

Pat Hale comments: In 2016, then-US Poet Laureate Juan Felipe Herrera led a workshop in which we created cave drawings, and from them, wrote legends. "A Brief History of Everything" came out of that workshop pretty much verbatim. As I see it now, it expresses our need to listen to and learn from nature. Back then, the whole process felt like magic.

Dolores Hayden is the author of *Exuberance* (Red Hen), which was a Connecticut Book Award Finalist and a Foreword Indies Book Award Finalist for Poetry. Her poems appear in *The Yale Review*, *Poetry*, *The Best American Poetry*, *Poetry Daily*, and *Verse Daily*. She's received awards from the Poetry Society of America and the New England Poetry Club, and residencies from VCCA, Djerassi, and the Center for Book Arts. Professor emerita at Yale, she lives in Guilford.

Joan Hofmann is a member of the Executive Board of Riverwood Poetry. She was the first Poet Laureate of Canton, Connecticut (2015-2019). Her poems have been published in anthologies, journals, and three chapbooks: *Coming Back*, *Alive*, and *Alive, Too*. When not hiking, she often walks along the Farmington River near her home in Collinsville, or watches the house being built on the lot in "The Takedown."

Susan Kinsolving's books are *Peripheral Vision*, *The White Eyelash*, *Dailies & Rushes*, a finalist for The National Book Critics Circle Award, and *Among Flowers*. Her poems have received critical acclaim from *The New York Times*, *New Yorker*, *Poetry*, *The Wall Street Journal*, *Vanity Fair*, and *Publishers Weekly*. As a guest poet, she has appeared in many venues, nationally and internationally.

Frederick-Douglass Knowles II is an educator and activist fervent in achieving community augmentation through literary arts. He is the author of *BlackRoseCity*, and a Professor of English at Three Rivers Community College in Norwich, Connecticut and serves as the inaugural Poet Laureate for the

City of Hartford. He is a recipient of the Nutmeg Poetry Award, and the 2020 Connecticut of The Arts Fellow in Artist Excellence for Poetry/Creative Non-Fiction.

Elizabeth Kudlacz is a scientist and poet living and working in Groton, Connecticut. While daily reveling in the natural wonders found in her small yard, she occasionally travels further afield to be astonished by other fellow earth-citizens such as the gray whales that migrate annually to protected bays off Baja California. Her poetry has been published in *Aurorean, Bellowing Ark, Cicada, Connecticut River Review, Freshwater* and *Haibun Today* in addition to several anthologies.

Susannah Lawrence lives in the old hills of northwestern Connecticut. A long-time environmental activist, she knows there is always more to do. Her collection, *Just Above the Bone*, appeared in 2016. Publication credits include *The Ekphrastic Review, The Comstock Review, The Cortland Review, Green Hills Literary Lantern, The MacGuffin, Nimrod, Poet Lore* and a recent anthology, *The Monday Poets*.

David K. Leff is an award-winning essayist and poet, and former deputy commissioner of the Connecticut Department of Environmental Protection. He is the author of a dozen books, including two novels in verse. David is the Canton, Connecticut Poet Laureate. In 2016-2017 he was appointed by the National Park Service to serve as poet-in-residence for the New England National Scenic Trail.

Jeanne LeVasseur is professor emeritus at Quinnipiac University. She is the author of a book of poetry entitled *Planetary Nights*. Her poetry has been published in *Nimrod, The Iowa Review, Yankee, The American Journal of Nursing, Literature and Medicine*, and *JAMA*, among other journals. Her poems have appeared in six anthologies, including *Between the Heartbeats: Poetry and Prose by Nurses* and *Intensive Care: Poetry by Nurses*.

Laura Mazza-Dixon, author of *Forged by Joy,* comments: The poem "Acqua Alta" began with a discovery five years ago of the essay "Ornithology at St. Mark's" in the April 1917 issue of *The Auk*. The praise that author J.A. Farley bestowed on the faithful depiction of birds in the mosaics came back to mind with the news of the flooding of St. Mark's in Venice last year.

Rennie McQuilkin served as Connecticut Poet Laureate from 2015-2018. He co-founded the Sunken Garden Poetry Festival, which he directed for 9 years. His poetry has appeared in *The Atlantic, Poetry, The American*

Scholar, *The Southern Review*, *The Yale Review*, *The Hudson Review*, and other publications. The author of several poetry collections, he has received a number of awards, including fellowships from the NEA and the Connecticut Commission on the Arts, the Connecticut Center for the Book's Lifetime Achievement Award, and its 2010 poetry award.

Lisa Meserole comments: Of all my world travels, these steps I took not far from home, in the firefly-lit dark, are some of the most beautiful I've ever experienced. I'm grateful to Bill and Mary Ellen McDonald for their stewardship, for sharing their love and knowledge of fireflies with me, and to Linda Bisbee for leading me there.

Amy Nawrocki is the author of six poetry collections. She is the recipient of numerous awards including honors from The Hamden Arts Commission, The Connecticut Poetry Society, New Millennium Writings, and The Connecticut Center for the Book. Her most recent collection, *Mouthbrooders*, was a finalist for the 2020 Connecticut Book Award.

Marilyn Nelson taught English at the University of Connecticut from 1978 to 2002. She was recently elected to the Board of Chancellors of the Academy of American Poets. Nelson was appointed as State Poet Laureate by the Connecticut Commission on the Arts in 2001, and she served for five years in that honorary position.

Tom Nicotera is the coordinator of Bloomfield Library's Wintonbury Poetry Series, and he produces the annual "Celebrate Bloomfield" Poetry Event featuring 17 Bloomfield poets. Nicotera is a mentor for the American School for the Deaf poetry collaboration with Greater Hartford Academy of the Arts. His poetry book, *What Better Place to Be Than Here?* was published by Foothills Publishing in 2015.

Patricia Horn O'Brien is Poet Laureate of Old Saybrook, Connecticut, a member of the Guilford Poetry Guild, and co-founder of Connecticut River Poets. She's facilitated poetry workshops, including at York C.I. hospice program and at Middlesex and Asnuntuck Community Colleges. O'Brien recently published her first book of poetry, *When Less Than Perfect is Enough*. Her memoir, *The Laughing Rabbit: A Mother, a Son, and the Ties that Bind*, written with her son, Richard, chronicles their story of adoption and reunion.

Lana Orphanides is the author of *Searching for Angels*, published by Anthem Press, and the chapbook, *Sea and the Sound of Wind, Poem of Greece*. She participated in Poetry of the Wild where poems were posted both in natural settings and public spaces. and has done readings throughout Connecticut. Orphanides is a member of the Connecticut River Poets and Poets for the Planet.

Julia Paul is president of Riverwood Poetry Series, a long-standing reading series in Hartford, Connecticut. Her poetry has appeared or is forthcoming in literary journals, both national and international, as well as in several anthologies, including *From Under the Bridges of America* and *Forgotten Women*. Paul is the author of a chapbook, *Staring Down the Tracks* (The Poetry Box, 2020) and a book, *Shook* (Grayson Books, 2018). She served as Manchester, Connecticut's first Poet Laureate and is an elder law attorney.

Jennifer A. Payne is a poet, writer, and spiritual ecologist. Payne is the author of several books including *LOOK UP! Musings on the Nature of Mindfulness, Evidence of Flossing: What We Leave Behind,* and the chapbook *Waiting Out the Storm.* She is a member of the Guilford Poets Guild, creator/editor of *MANIFEST (zine)*, and writes regularly on her blog: www.randomactsofwriting.net.

Michael "Chief" Peterson marries social consciousness with mellow poetic verses. Born and raised in New Britain, Peterson is the playwright of and actor in his one-man show, *I Wish Life Had Training Wheels.* He was recently appointed as the first ever Poet Laureate of his hometown, New Britain Connecticut. He is a three-time Connecticut Spoken Word Grand Slam Champion. Peterson is Dean of Students at New Britain High School, and is also a part-time Child Development Specialist. From the high school where he works to the stages where he performs, this poet on the rise is about turning his art into action and inspiring people to do the same.

Pit Pinegar is the author of three volumes of poetry. She has a long history of animal rescue going back to childhood when her dad, a physician, assisted. The rescue in "One" was a different experience: boundaries dissolved, that tiny lizard became the center of the universe, he and I a single filament in the same gorgeous and endangered whole.

Charles Rafferty has two books forthcoming in 2021: a collection of stories called *Somebody Who Knows Somebody* (Gold Wake Press) and a collection of prose poems called *A Cluster of Noisy Planets* (BOA Editions). Currently, he co-directs the MFA program at Albertus Magnus College and teaches at the Westport Writers' Workshop.

Lorraine Riess is a member of Connecticut River Poets, where she participates in group readings at local venues. Her work has appeared in publications and anthologies in the shoreline area. Her first collection of poems is due to be published in 2021. She is the current Poet Laureate of Haddam, CT. *Contact: lcfriess@att.net*

Clare Rossini serves as Artist-in-Residence at Trinity College in Hartford, teaching creative writing courses and directing an outreach program which places college students in Hartford public school art classrooms. She comments: When researching extinct bird species one warm spring day—a melancholy task!—I came across Cornell's University's Macaulay Library archive, the world's largest collection of digitized wildlife sounds. My office window was wide open. The rest is in the poem.

Maria Sassi is a prize-winning poet and playwright. Her book of poems *Rooted in Stars*, was accepted by the Beinecke Rare Book and Manuscript Library at Yale University. Her prize-winning video, *Five Ocean Poems*, was complete with a grant from the Harford Foundation for Public Giving. Sassi led poetry workshops for nine years at the Hartford College for Women, University of Hartford, and she has studied with the Pulitzer Prize winning poet and translator Richard Wilbur.

Alexandrina Sergio is author of three poetry collections: *My Daughter is Drummer in the Rock 'n Roll Band*, *That's How the Light Gets In*, and *Old Is Not a Four-Letter Word* (Antrim House). Her work has been widely published in journals and anthologies and has been nominated for a Pushcart Prize. Sergio served from 2015-2018 as Glastonbury's first Poet Laureate.

Pegi Deitz Shea is the author of more than 450 published articles, essays, and poems for adult readers and young readers, and she's a two-time winner of the Connecticut Book Award. She teaches in the University of Connecticut Creative Writing Program. Shea founded and directs the Poetry Rocks reading series in Vernon, Connecticut, where she is Poet Laureate.

Vivian Shipley is the CSU Distinguished Professor and has taught at Southern Connecticut State University since 1969. Her 12th book of poetry, *An Archaeology of Days*, was published in 2019 by Negative Capability Press and was nominated for the Pulitzer Prize and named a 2019-2020 Paterson Poetry Prize Finalist. She was awarded a 2021 Connecticut Office of the Arts Artist Fellowship for Poetry. *The Poet* (La Lit Press at SLU) and *Perennial* (Negative Capability Press, Mobile, ALA) were published in 2015.

John L. Stanizzi is the author of *Ecstasy Among Ghosts, Sleepwalking, Dance Against the Wall, After the Bell, Hallelujah Time! High Tide – Ebb Tide, Four Bits, Chants, Sundowning,* and *POND*. His work has been translated into Italian and appeared widely in Italy. His nonfiction has been published in various journals. A former New England Poet of the Year, and Wesleyan University Etherington Scholar, Stanizzi teaches literature at Manchester Community College in Connecticut, and lives with his wife, Carol, in Coventry.

Steve Straight's books include *The Almanac* (Curbstone/Northwestern University Press, 2012) and *The Water Carrier* (Curbstone, 2002). He was professor of English and director of the poetry program at Manchester Community College, in Connecticut.

Sarah P. Strong is the author of two novels and two books of poetry, including *The Mouth of Earth* (University of Nevada Press, 2020), an exploration of human response to the climate emergency. Their work has appeared in *The Nation, The Sun, The Southern Review, Poetry Daily,* and elsewhere. They live in Hamden, Connecticut and teach creative writing at Central Connecticut State University.

John Surowiecki has published seven chapbooks and five full collections of poetry; the most recent, *Martha Playing Wiffle Ball in Her Wedding Gown and Other Poems* (Encircle), was a finalist for last year's Connecticut Book Award. He has received the Poetry Foundation Pegasus Award for verse drama, the 2017 Nilson Prize for a First Novel, the Nimrod Pablo Neruda Prize, the Washington Prize, a Connecticut Poetry Fellowship, and the silver medal in the Sunken Garden National Competition.

Katherine Szpekman writes from her home in Collinsville, Connecticut. Her poetry is forthcoming in *Rockvale Review* and the *Connecticut Literary Anthology 2020*, and has appeared in *Red Eft Review, Sky Island Journal, Muddy River Poetry Review, Chestnut Review, Sheila-Na-Gig, Hiram Poetry Review,* and other publications. She was awarded Honorable Mention in the Connecticut River Review Poetry Contest 2019.

Elizabeth Tomanio writes poetry to better understand the world and herself in it. She won first place in the Love Tanka Contest sponsored by West Hartford Libraries. Her poetry resides online and in print within *Please See Me, Snapdragon: A Journal of Art & Healing, Caesura 2020* and the upcoming 2021 Anthology: *Night Forest* (Flying Ketchup Press).

Edwina Trentham is a Professor Emerita of English at Asnuntuck Community College in Enfield, Connecticut, where she founded the poetry journal, *Freshwater*. She was also a Visiting Instructor in the Graduate Liberal Studies Program at Wesleyan University. She has been a fellow at Yaddo and has published her work in a number of anthologies and periodicals. Her poetry collection, *Stumbling into the Light*, was published by Antrim House. She is a member of Connecticut River Poets and Poets for the Planet. Visit her website: edwinatrentham.com.

Davyne Verstandig is a University of Connecticut English professor Emerita, and a writing consultant. She has served as Poet Laureate of Washington, Connecticut and as justice of the peace. Her publications include work in *Pieces of the Whole, Provisions, Sex and Sexuality in a Feminist World, Songs of the Marrow Bone, Where Beach Meets Ocean, This One Has No Name, Laureates of Connecticut: An Anthology of Contemporary Poetry*. mymindisintheink@gmail.com.

Rhonda M. Ward the first Poet Laureate of New London, Connecticut, has organized poetry events in southeastern Connecticut since 2003. Her poems have appeared widely in print and online. Appearances include the University of Massachusetts at Dartmouth, Bowery Poetry Club, Arts Café Mystic, and the International Women's Arts Festival in Cumbria, UK. Rhonda has collaborated with visual artists for numerous projects including *The Question* with artist/activist Pamela Pike Gordinier and *Poetry of the Wild* with Connecticut artists Ana Flores and Diane Barcelo. She spent a month in Bulgaria through the Griffis Foundation Arts Exchange Program.

Christie Max Williams is a writer and actor who lives in Mystic, Connecticut. He has worked on stage, film, and TV in California, New York, and Connecticut, and also as a fruit vendor in Paris, a salmon fisherman in Alaska, a consultant on Wall Street, a writer for the National Audubon Society, and in leadership posts for non-profits. He co-founded and for many years directed The Arts Café Mystic. Williams' poems have won prizes and recognition in several prestigious competitions.

Elaine Zimmerman comments: The Tohoku earthquake triggered a tsunami. Their combined force disabled the power supply and cooling mechanisms of Fukushima Daiichi nuclear reactors. Three units of the plant were destroyed. Radioactive iodine, strontium and cesium entered soil and water. "Nothing Is Still in this World" tries to be inside the moment when the earth turned upside, life stopped for many, and radioactive elements cupped growth.

Permissions

Our thanks go to the following publishers, who first printed some of these poems. Every effort was made to gather previous publication credits; we apologize for any errors or omissions.

"Ashford Oak" by Denise Abercrombie from *The Chronicle*, Willimantic, Connecticut, January 4, 2020.

"For Berta Cáceres" and "The Call of the Void" by Jonathan Andersen both appeared in *Augur*, Red Dragonfly Press, 2018.

"Calling the Owl" by Terry Bohnhorst Blackhawk first appeared in *Yankee Magazine*, December, 1996, and later in the author's collection *body & field*, Michigan State University Press, 1999.

"Hand Tilling" by Aaron Caycedo-Kimura was previously published in *Here: a poetry journal*, 2018, Eastern Connecticut State University.

"Forage" by Luisa Caycedo-Kimura first appeared in *The Cincinnati Review*, Fall, 2019.

"Luna Moths" by Robert Cording was first published in *The Southern Review* and then in the author's book, *Walking with Ruskin*, CavanKerry Press, 2010.

"Walking with Ruskin" by Robert Cording was first published *The Georgia Review* and then in *Walking with Ruskin*, CavanKerry Press, 2010.

"Snapshot: Four Turkeys at the Feeder" by Daniel Donaghy was previously published in *Valparaiso Poetry Review*.

"Irrevocable" by Margaret Gibson first appeared in *The Gettysburg Review*, 2020.

"Not Children" by Benjamin S. Grossberg first appeared in *Mid-American Review* and then in *Sweet Core Orchard*, University of Tampa Press, 2009.

"Catawba" by Benjamin S. Grossberg first appeared in *The Kenyon Review* and then in *My Husband Would*, University of Tampa Press, 2020.

"A Brief History of Everything" by Pat Hale was previously published in *Naugatuck River Review*, Winter/Spring 2017.

"In the Middle Lane, Leaving New Haven" by Dolores Hayden appeared in *The Yale Review*, 2012.

"Christmas Eve Afternoon at Braddock Bay" by Rennie McQuilkin was originally published in *Here: A Poetry Journal*, Issue 2, 2018.

"Arboriculture" by Amy Nawrocki was originally published in *Four Blue Eggs*, Homebound Publications, 2014.

"But-Heads" by Marilyn Nelson was previously published on the website eco-poetry.org.

"Getting to Prayer" by Patricia Horn O'Brien first appeared in the *Our Changing Environment*, the Guilford Poets Guild 20th Anniversary Anthology.

"The Song of the Dusky Seaside Sparrow" by Clare Rossini first appeared in *The Kenyon Review*.

"Rare Grasses" by Maria Sassi was published previously in her book of the same name, *Rare Grasses*, Antrim House, 2015.

"Trespasser at Morgan Point" by Vivian Shipley was previously published in the author's collection *An Archeology of Days*, Negative Capability Press, 2019.

"The Trembling" by John Stanizzi first appeared in The Chronicle's *Here in Windham: A Celebration of Poets*.

"Cruising" by Steve Straight was previously published in *Plum Tree Tavern*.

"Anthropocene Birthday" by Sarah P. Strong first appeared in the author's poetry collection *The Mouth of Earth*, University of Nevada Press, 2020.

"Nothing Is Still in This World" by Elaine Zimmerman first appeared in Theodate, 2016, and later in *The Hartford Courant's* "CT Poet's Corner," 2020.

CPSIA information can be obtained
at www.ICGtesting.com
Printed in the USA
FSHW012131130221